Rock Jocks Wall Rats and Hang Dogs

Rock Climbing on the Edge of Reality

John Long

A RICHARD BALLANTINE/BYRON PREISS BOOK

A FIRESIDE BOOK
PUBLISHED BY SIMON & SCHUSTER
NEW YORK LONDON TORONTO SYDNEY TOKYO SINGAPORE

FIRESIDE
Rockefeller Center
1230 Avenue of the Americas
New York, New York 10020

FIRESIDE and colophon are registered trademarks
of Simon & Schuster Inc.

Manufactured in the United States of America

10 9 8 7 6 5 4 3 2 1

Library of Congress Cataloging-in-Publication Data

Long, John, 1954–
    Rock jocks, wall rats and hang dogs : rock climbing on the edge
of reality / John Long.
            p.   cm.
    "A Fireside book."
    1. Rock climbing.   2. Rock climbing—United States.   I. Title.
GV200.2.L667   1994
796.5′223—dc20   94-6416
                                                                 CIP

ISBN: 0-671-88466-2

There are only three sports—
mountain climbing, bullfighting, and motor racing—
all others being games.

—Ernest Hemingway

Introduction

A young man, barely twenty, runs his fingers over a one-foot section of crack. So zeroed in is his face that his mother would not recognize him. His eyes shift to the dozens of pitons, wedges and assorted widgets hanging on slings draped over each shoulder. From this tackle he must select and fill a bit of the crack with something sufficient to support his 180 pounds. *Everything* hangs on the precision of his choice. The crack is not much, like the crease in a sidewalk.

A thunderbolt could not break his focus, though his awareness rolls out like the rings formed by a pebble dropped into a pond. He is keenly aware of standing in nylon slings connected to a dime-sized steel piton, hammered into the crack at knee level. He knows that if the piton goes, it's trouble: The nearest piton that can break his fall is 60 feet below him. He feels the rope that runs from his harness down through dozens of marginal pitons and bits of copper and aluminum swedges that, over the last five hours, he has pasted into the incipient crack with an 18-ounce hammer and a prayer. He knows the rope ends 130 feet below, where his partner carefully tends the line, ready to lock it off if he pops. He can feel the slight weight of the haul line clipped to the back of his harness, and knows that it never touches the overhanging wall as it describes a lazy loop through midair, ending at a knot on top of the 150-pound haul bag, moored to the same six-piton anchor his partner is tethered to, seemingly a continent away. His knows there is food and water in the haul bag, likewise the hammock he will sleep in tonight, lashed to the face of the rock. There are no signs of ledges above. He feels every inch of the remaining 800 feet soaring overhead like a great gray wave. But he knows no more than what he can see, for no one has ever climbed this section of the wall. He's dead reckoning. It's been heavy weather the whole way up.

As to the 2,200 feet of vertical rock below him, he knows everything, for he and his partner have spent the last five days leap-frogging up it, one piton and three feet at a time, sometimes taking eight hours and several falls to master a single, 165-foot rope length. There has not been a ledge to stand on for the three days they have covered a span of rock steeper and larger than the Empire State Building. The memory of accidentally dropping a sling and watching it free-fall 2,000 feet before it struck the lower-angled slabs is burned into his mind. Occasional flashes of fear and loneliness, strong as they are, cannot pierce his focus; but what he can't acknowledge, he feels turning deep in his belly.

He is aware that the section of rock 18 inches before his eyes is an infinitesimal bit of the biggest chunk of exposed granite in the world: El Capitan. He has revered that name since he was fifteen years old, when he'd fall asleep thinking about it, only to have the thoughts meld into dreams of his climbing it. Now, as he meticulously hammers another copper swedge into the crack, clips an aluminum snaplink through it, and the rope through that, finally clipping in a nylon stirrup and gingerly stepping a few feet higher, holding his breath and praying the swedge won't suddenly rip out, it is impossible for him to separate his dreams of climbing El Capitan with the actual deed. The scale of his journey and the pressing nearness of his condition surpass his own view, the emotions too many and too potent to do anything but experience. There is no yesterday, no tomorrow, just the electric now, and the fragile copper swedge supporting his weight, and the hammering in his chest, and the realization that half a mile up a wall of naked rock, life and death have merged.

The reasons he is climbing are deeper than words can go. He only knows that it is not desire or even skill that keeps him moving, but obligation. He *has* to climb this "big wall." The reasons, whenever stated, never sound quite right, and only matter to nonclimbers anyway. To him, what matters is that this copper swedge holds, and the next one after that, all the way to the summit, still two days away, maybe three.

There, he and his partner will sit on the brink of giant rock and wait for the world to catch back up to them. Dangling their legs off the lip and gazing down into the valley nearly 4,000 feet below, shadows will migrate across the green meadow, and the complex grays and blacks and oranges on Middle Cathedral, a mile across the valley, will capture them. If they keep watching these things, can remember them acutely, they will never be without food for thought and will never be truly alone.

Their strength, their desires, the meager food and water they shared this last week were all necessary for existence in the first instance. But El Capitan, nearly three quarters of a mile high and five times as wide, and the valley spread out far below them, are extras. The smell of the trees and the knife-cut profiles of the big rocks and the red panorama of the western sky are an embellishment of life, not a condition of it. Only the rarest things give extras, so the young men have much to hope for from the perch they sit on and the valley they gaze down at.

Yosemite Valley is a point of light, a claustrophobic gulch, a jazz riff, a thunderclap, a pool of rainwater, a social vacuum and a wonder of the world. Yosemite is Jeffrey pines, solemn gray dawns and emerald meadows, double-decker tour busses, ten thousand campfires and twice as many tourists. To the climber, Yosemite Valley is all these things and a thousand more; but above all, Yosemite is about climbing rocks. Titanic rocks.

For twenty-five years, Yosemite was the sanctum sanctorum of world rock climbing, the ideal against which the French Alps, the Dolomites and a thousand lesser areas were measured. Countless climbers hauled the same dream to the small national park in central California, and no matter how many stories they'd read, or photos or books or movies they had seen of Yosemite, they brought with them a narrower vision than their first glimpse of the "big walls."

The sides of the valley, though steep, are uneven and craggy. Sometimes they rear nearly a mile above the valley floor. Trees and scrub cling to some parts; other parts are sectioned and terraced. At intervals, and standing out bold and detached from this backdrop, are beetling spires, soaring arêtes and faces of polished rock, each one singular in form and a monument to itself: Middle Cathedral, a great tinctured fist nearly 3,000 feet high; Sentinel, rising 2,000 feet off the scree like a mighty gray tombstone; Half Dome's cleft North Face, the face of a billion postcards, veiled in ancient shade; and the crown jewel of American rock climbing, El Capitan. Soaring straight up off the talus, its great white slabs, orange towers and sheer magnitude seem terrible, though less so than the terrible emptiness that sets in a climber's gut the first time he sees it.

Looming on both sides of a valley barely a mile wide, these walls seem to press in on a rookie with all the chilling mass of the great glacier that first formed them. Yet the climbers came: Germans in flannel knickers and alpine hats; Frenchmen in mountain boots and red scarves; working-class Brits, or "Limies," looking for a fight or another beer, their skin so pale you'd swear they'd grown up in a closet; Australians tough as dingos and ready for anything so long as there was risk involved; Japanese, each with flags of the rising sun on their tottering packs, on their shirts, tied round their heads, asking little more from life but a chance to risk it; Mexicans poor as dirt and fearless as God; Italians, none of whom spoke word one of English, but whose naked passion was vouchsafed by their waving hands and the much repeated "Fantastico!" And us Americans, ex–center fielders and running backs, no counts, bastards and cast offs, from Los Angeles and upstate New York, from Boulder, Colorado, and Waco, Texas. And every climber stayed in Camp 4, traditional outdoor flophouse for anyone with the dream, a rope and a restless spirit.

After graduating from high school in 1971, I jumped on a Greyhound and chugged up for the first of many summers in Camp 4. The moment I entered that small, boulder-strewn campground, staggering under the load of three duffel bags, I passed through the looking glass and left my past behind forever. I met people there, people just like me and nothing like me, people who spoke not a word of English, yet their hearts spoke my language exactly. I lived with these people, and I shared meals and campsites, I fought, climbed, suffered, laughed, cried and competed with these people and had the times of my life.

Most of us were young and full of fool notions, so more than anything, we learned that all Frenchman were not epicene little Pierres with berets and pencil 'stashes; that all Germans were not Nazis; that some Swiss couldn't yodel and some Argentineans couldn't ride a stallion; that Sandy Koufax wasn't the only Jewish athlete; that some were climbers just as young and busted as I was and just as crazy. Here, any rules were self-imposed. Everyone was free to invent himself as he saw fit, since no one was climbing for country or race or creed, but for themselves. In the process, the Yosemite climber discovered the whole business was as much about Camp 4 as about the skin and sleepless nights lost on the big rocks.

European climbers were better off than we Americans, with their Day-Glo tents and immaculate campsites and big Coleman stoves and coolers—and even secondhand cars in the parking lot. Most American climbers were like I was, barely out of high school and flat broke. Few of us owned tents, so often there was just a thin Ensolite pad or a poncho or sometimes nothing at all between our sleeping bags, the dirt we slept on and the stars above. All that we owned, and some things we didn't, were strung high in trees to thwart hungry bears. It was said that Jim Pettigrew caught a brown bear stealing dried apricots from his tent, that he lassoed it with an 8-millimeter haul rope, and was dragged all the way to Fresno. Layton Kor was supposed to have wrestled a local bear named "Tiny," who was "about the size of a Volkswagen, only much bigger." A Spanish climber was rumored to have had his arm ripped off by a grizzly (there are no grizzlies in Yosemite), only to have it sewn back on that same night by Scottish climber/surgeon Tom Patey. It is not known why Pettigrew never let go of the rope, if Kor pinned Tiny, or if the Spaniard ever climbed again, because all of these stories were flat lies; but they added a wild footnote to the place and to the climbers who lived there.

We had no sensitivity at all concerning Yosemite as regarded by Ansel Adams or John Muir or anyone but fellow climbers. Only in the mythology of the dream (and we considered ourselves the only rightful players) did the valley figure significantly for us, and here it took on a glorious cast: For Yosemite Valley was the epicenter of world rock climbing, and was therefore the center of the universe. Here it was possible to master the great rock walls and soften our budding awareness of how small and insignificant we really were. It was all of a piece: the peanut butter dinners, the pissants, the thieving squirrels, the army sleeping bags and the lumpy ground, moonlight leaking down through dark and towering pine trees and, of course, the dreams and nightmares of starting up El Capitan the next morning.

That was what lured us to Yosemite—the need to climb El Capitan, or another of the legendary rocks. If you succeeded, you could do anything, the thinking went, and it would go far in patching things up with Dad, who'd demanded you work the summer as a law clerk or a gas station attendant or something, *anything* "worthwhile." You'd refused, of course, and that led to a blowout. And you'd left home on bad terms. Later came the splashy magazines, coffee table books and network television specials on climbing, and the public's slow acceptance of the "Sport of Kings" as viable. But this was 1971, and things were different.

There was no raving crowd in those early days, no wannabes, no glory outside the slim ranks of your peers. Even the adventure world largely ignored climbing. Climbing is first and always a participant's sport, so there is little money in it. Young climbers would work the most wretched jobs through the winter—freezing their asses off on a Wyoming oil rig, pounding nails and ducking bullets for "big money" ($120 a day, while you lasted) in El Salvador, digging trenches wherever—to raise just enough cash to pass the next summer in the valley. Of course, the whole business is indefensible from without because climbing has always been an individual experience, nearly impossible to render true on paper. Not everyone feels a need for a baptism of fire, or wants to take part in a direct deed that gives them an immediate feeling of life and death. Yet the jeopardy and the supposed romance are usually overstated, and in fact it's the subtle little things words can never get at that I cling to now. But there was nothing subtle about getting hurt, the flip side of the dream.

Every year a few of those who came to Yosemite would die there. News of a death or a bad fall washed through Camp 4 like an angry squall, then everything froze in a terrible silence. You would gaze at the empty tent that no one would ever return to, a dozen fragments of a young man's history strewn beneath the rain fly—a soccer ball, a fly rod, a dog-eared paperback with a name scrawled across the cover in felt pen. You couldn't say anything worth a damn to the victim's other friends—milling about the campsite, dazed by these reminders and the vacuum created by the absence—but sometimes you had to try.

In that dim hang point between sleep and wakefulness I

sometimes see myself, nineteen years old, in the shade of
the great pines, staring at the ground as I broke the news to
the wife of a Welsh climber I hardly knew. I'd been on the
rescue, or body recovery, and just afterward, when she
rushed up to me in camp, the thankless job was mine: "Ian
has died in a climbing accident." The words tumbled from
my mouth like the falling rocks that had killed him, and
were killing me. Her hands came up to her face and she
backpedaled away, glaring at me as though I'd killed him
myself, I and all the others who'd shared his dream.
"Meaningless. It's all so meaningless," she kept repeating.
Her voice was hollow and came from the end of the world,
from the future, from all the empty years in front of her
and from her first night alone in the tent.

But for all those who hauled the dream there from parts
unknown, the future had no meaning at all without climbing. For better or for worse, the dream was as old and as
staunch as the big rocks, and in an hour or a day, someone
would stumble back into camp with a fantastic tale of victory and the balance was restored, no matter how torn and
empty you felt about the loss. Like the memories, the game
at the top was for keeps.

Of course, this is not representative of all climbing, or
even a small part of climbing—just the radical end of it.
But it's at the extreme end that the most remarkable things
happen, and it's the flavor of the extreme that keeps the
climber going back to the cliff side.

Climbing changes people—be it on a boulder or a 50-
foot high quarry—but particularly on routes that may
take days to accomplish. Climbing a big wall is an event
that dominates your life as only nature can dominate the
lives of men and women. When there is danger and you
have to deal with it not for twelve rounds, or four quar-

ters, but for a week at a go, it will leave a clear mark on you for life.

During my first few summers in Camp 4, I'd return from a long climb to find boys I'd left for a couple of days suddenly changed. A single big wall—slugging their way up Half Dome, battling thunderstorms and "sleeping" in slings, soaking wet and hating life—had hurtled them far beyond themselves. Their youth lay behind them like snakes' skins, and their faces had set overnight. Some had finally become sufficient unto themselves; others had seen some private demon die in the epic, and what survived had won a new beginning; still others had confirmed the value of their life by almost losing it. Whatever the reasons, they didn't need climbing anymore, and so left the valley for good.

I finally left for these reasons and others: My elbows had tendonitis, I was sick of being broke, and I craved to break out of a radiant arroyo named Yosemite and see the big world. All of it. I was off to Vanuatu, river-running in Borneo, caving in Irian Jaya, wild things and wilder places whose names I could never get my tongue around. Without knowing it, I was all along searching for the intensity I used to feel climbing in the valley. After ten years of globe-trotting, I finally realized I would never find that fiendish intensity again—until I tie back into a rope.

Part One

It was 1969 and I was fourteen, living in a suburb east of Los Angeles. I'd just seen *The Mountain*, where a plane crashes on an icy plateau, and Spencer Tracy skis in through a snowstorm, flakes out the rope, grabs his pickax and conducts a magnificent rescue. And my mom had an issue of *National Geographic* featuring climbers in the Utah desert scaling a needle of brown rock, slim as a flagpole. I really wanted to learn all those rope shenanigans. But *how*? I rode my bike to the library and started digging.

There were no climbing manuals in the stacks, but an encyclopedia had a couple of pages dedicated to the subject, including a full-page illustration of an enormous marine clinging to a soggy cliff. Ropes and cords were coming off him from all directions, his body swaddled with all kinds of spikes and daggers and things I had never seen before. One look at that marine and I knew I'd never understand what he was up to, and could never afford the tackle even if I did.

About a month later, a man named John Goddard showed up at our high school. He'd kayaked down the Blue Nile, trekked across Afghanistan, penetrated the darkest regions of the Amazon. There was talk that he'd eaten human flesh, and his crude home movies and embroidered lectures enchanted me. For about three months I hitchhiked all over Southern California, following Goddard on his lecture circuit, hounding him backstage after every show. I got to know the man in a casual way, and copied his every move, even down to the way he spit. Like many kids raised in a cozy little suburb, everything was ordered and confined and geared to make life soft and easy. Dead bored and jumpy as a cricket, I couldn't get enough of Goddard's world. When I discovered he wore a toupee and drove a Sedan de Ville, his image suffered; but I continued spending weekends thrashing about the scrubby little mountains above our town, looking for my own Amazon.

I'd snag a friend off my baseball team, toss two days' worth of canned goods into a canvas army backpack, and head out cross-country. Soon we were marching through groves of poison sumac and stinging nettles, thrashing up brushy riverbeds, scrambling over moraine slopes and through brief forests charred black by annual fires, finally emerging above the tree line scraped, punctured, swollen, black as chimney sweeps. The mountains above my hometown were piss poor.

Eventually, I hooked up with another kid named Robles, who had boundless energy and the weak smile of the original fool, and who shared my same lust to get out of town. So we started trekking around the local mountains together, progressively tackling more direct lines up the local peaks, taking a 50-foot yachting line along for protection on the tougher stretches of vertical dirt and manzanita. We were inspired by the crackpot version of climbing served up on the big screen—the bold mountaineer teetering on a slim shelf below blank rock. He hurls the grappling hook, and though its purchase is something less than a frozen cobweb, he hand-walks up the line like it's tied off to a tugboat stanchion. A bad example to follow, and it's a miracle neither of us was killed for trying to.

The plan, and we always had a plan, was simple: We'd bone up on local fare for another year, or until one of us could drive, then we'd go climb the Matterhorn, then on to Everest. There was still the problem of not understanding what the hell the marine was up to in that encyclopedia, or what all the doodads were about or how the knots and confusing ropes were rigged. We figured to hone the fine points once we got to Switzerland. We were both fifteen.

I spent that summer working in a gas station and playing baseball. Now sixteen, I was torn. From about the age of eight on, baseball, and the desire to play in the major leagues, had dominated my life. It's a common enough dream, but with the distance of time, I realize what a strange dream it really was, and what a strange piece of work it was growing up. First we fought imaginary Indians in our backyard. Then we got toy pistols and "killed" anything moving. Later we took to fistfights, really wicked ones. Finally, a man stuck a piece of lumber in our hands and told us to bash a hardball somebody was chucking at our heads. I loved the game, but loafing around center field, my mind started drifting down wild rivers and into unexplored jungle and up Mount Everest. And then one day, in the local backpacking shop, I saw a handwritten flyer from the Granite Mountain Guide Service offering classes in rock climbing—for $20. I ripped the note off the bulletin board, raced home and called Sandy Gaines, Chief Guide—and *only* guide—for the Granite Mountain Guide Service.

I had three other friends who were provisionally interested in climbing, and before my first lesson, we got together and drew up a fresh plan. They would contribute $5 each, I would go off with Sandy Gaines, risk my life to learn the fundamentals, and if I survived, would pass on the knowledge and we'd form a climbing club and go to Everest that fall. No sense in fiddling around on the Matterhorn after going to Joshua Tree, we reasoned. I never saw their $5.

The night before my first lesson, my father pulled out various road maps and we went over the route to Joshua Tree National Monument, then drove down to the gas station and checked the tires, the spare, the radiator and gassed up. Back home, the old man told me to listen carefully to the instructor and not to drive like I played baseball, which was recklessly.

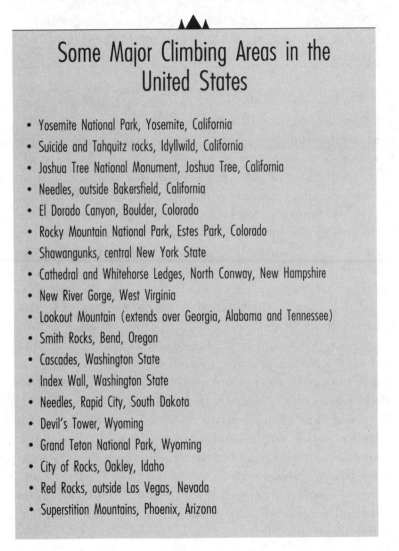

Some Major Climbing Areas in the United States

- Yosemite National Park, Yosemite, California
- Suicide and Tahquitz rocks, Idyllwild, California
- Joshua Tree National Monument, Joshua Tree, California
- Needles, outside Bakersfield, California
- El Dorado Canyon, Boulder, Colorado
- Rocky Mountain National Park, Estes Park, Colorado
- Shawangunks, central New York State
- Cathedral and Whitehorse Ledges, North Conway, New Hampshire
- New River Gorge, West Virginia
- Lookout Mountain (extends over Georgia, Alabama and Tennessee)
- Smith Rocks, Bend, Oregon
- Cascades, Washington State
- Index Wall, Washington State
- Needles, Rapid City, South Dakota
- Devil's Tower, Wyoming
- Grand Teton National Park, Wyoming
- City of Rocks, Oakley, Idaho
- Red Rocks, outside Las Vegas, Nevada
- Superstition Mountains, Phoenix, Arizona

- Mt. Lemmon, Tucson, Arizona
- Granite Mountain, Prescott, Arizona
- Little Cottonwood Canyon (and environs), Salt Lake City, Utah
- Throughout the Four Corners (Utah, Colorado, Arizona and New Mexico) there are countless areas to find world-class desert climbing

The two-and-a-half-hour drive out to Joshua Tree was by far the longest solo drive of my life, a stretch I traveled at over 80 miles an hour. "Josh," as the monument is known to climbers, is a flat, arid sweep of high desert several hours east of L.A., peppered with scrub oak, datura, flowering yuccas and countless Joshua trees, their barbed, arthritic limbs twisted in bizarre attitudes. Strewn about the terrain are hundreds of bronzed rocks, from boulders to 300-foot-high monoliths, rearing from the landscape like huge tan fists. The entire area is a favorite haunt for drifters, gurus, psychics and UFO buffs—pretty sketchy society, but there's no denying the monument has an alien aspect to it. The sky is just a little bluer, the air a little sharper, the shadows a little harder than seems possible. In the following fifteen years, I would see Joshua Tree blossom into one of the most popular climbing areas in the world, the heartland of the climbing revolution.

I met Sandy Gaines at the Hidden Valley Campground. He had sandy hair, a sandy moustache, a sandy complexion—was altogether one of the sandiest men I'd ever seen. We immediately went over to the dark side of a big rock, and I cringed as Sandy dragged from his rucksack some of the spikes and clips that the marine had worn in that baffling illustration. But Sandy quickly explained that all the gear and forthcoming techniques were basic, requiring only a few outings to get "wired." We went over the knots (rock climbing rarely uses more than four basic knots), how to rig the swami belt (a lashing of nylon sling, wrapped around the waist, now abandoned in place of the more comfortable harnesses) and the basic belaying procedure. Then Sandy rigged me with hammer and holster and an over-the-shoulder cleaning sling, and started up a dark, vertical chute with a crack in the back of it.

▲▲▲

The System

The whole point of the rope and gear climbers employ is to safeguard them in the event of a fall. When the leader starts up a climb, the aim is to have fun, not to cheat death; and if he falls (which has become routine), he does not expect to get hurt, or even scratched.

In a nutshell: Two climbers are tied into their respective ends of a 165-foot rope (standard length). Starting from the ground, one climber secures himself ("anchors") to a tree, a big block, or perhaps arranges an anchor by fitting some of his specialized gear into a handy crack. In any case, his anchor must be fail-safe. Having decided on a particular passage, or "route" up the cliff—say a prominent crack—the other climber (the "leader") starts up, scaling the crack using hands and feet. Meanwhile, the man anchored on the ground (the "belayer") pays out the rope, using a technique or device that can stop the rope cold if need be.

Now the leader has reached a difficult section. He removes an appropriate piece of gear—normally a "nut," aka a "chock"—from his sling, places it in the crack, clips a "carabiner" (an aluminum snaplink with a spring-loaded gate) through the gear, then clips his rope through the carabiner. The leader now has an anchor that "protects" him for the climbing just overhead. How? Say he climbs three feet above the anchor and falls. The belayer checks the rope; the leader falls twice the distance he is above the anchor, or six feet. Since the rope stretches, he might fall inches more, but the belayer, who is holding the fall, doesn't budge. The leader, unscathed, gathers his wits and tries again.

You may ask: If the leader was three feet above the anchor, why did he fall six feet plus the odd extra inches? First, for several reasons, the belayer cannot effectively take in the rope when the leader falls. His duty is to lock the rope off, so when the leader's weight comes onto the rope, the rope is held fast. If the leader is three feet above his anchor—or "protection"—he must first fall three feet to that protection. He still has three feet of slack out, so he must fall three more feet, past the protection, for a total fall of six feet plus, depending on rope stretch. Hence the equation: The leader falls twice the distance above his last protection—and then some.

Carrying on, the leader places protection as he sees fit, always placing something before a hard section. Up until the early seventies, protection devices were almost exclusively pitons—steel spikes that were hammered into cracks in the rock. Since then, various alloy wedges and intricate camming devices have virtually replaced pitons as generic protection devices. These wedges and cams are fitted into hollows and constrictions in cracks, and when fallen upon, are actually further wedged into the rock.

Anyway, by the time the leader is 60 feet up the crack, he may have placed six or eight pieces of protection, depending on the difficulty and how secure he feels. Once the leader gains a convenient place to stop—say a ledge or a stout tree—he arranges a belay anchor that is absolutely fail-safe. In this case, that anchor must be strong enough that, no matter what the other climber does, no matter how far he falls, he cannot cause the anchor to fail or come out. Now it is the leader's turn to "belay," or take the rope in, as the "second" follows the "pitch," or rope length. As the second follows, he removes all the protection that the leader placed, so it may be used on the next pitch. Since the belayer takes in the rope as the second man on the rope ("follower") climbs up to him, the second can only fall as far as the rope stretches, usually a foot or so, and mere inches if little rope is out. Once the second reaches the leader's anchor, or "belay," he takes over the lead, while the erstwhile leader continues belaying. The process is continued until the team finishes the route.

This is known as free climbing. Note that the gear itself is not used to make upward progress: The leader does not hang from the gear that he places, rather he climbs using only hands and feet. In free climbing, the gear is used only to safeguard against a fall. The sport is to climb the rock using only your own physical abilities. Rope and gear are what make the process sane and allow you to push your limits, saving your life should you fall off. Since falling has become an integral part of the sport, both the system and the gear are reliable.

When the rock becomes too holdless or too steep to climb using hands and feet, the climber must resort to "direct aid" techniques. This entails the leader building himself a ladder of equipment up the wall, each piece supporting his entire weight—via nylon stirrups—as he moves up one piece and a few feet at a time. Direct aid is almost always required to scale any great wall of rock, which tends to be steep. More on this later.

My hands trembled as I realized I had Sandy's life in them, but as he splayed and chimneyed his way up the chute, I saw he did so with a much-practiced technique, that he flowed up the pitch as water might flow down it. His feet ratcheted out on opposing walls of the chute, Sandy stopped here and again to drive a piton, clipping the rope in with a carabiner, then carrying on without a word spoken. Right off, I understood that technical climbing was a matter of fitness and technique. But up above, where the crack ran out and the chute steepened, and Sandy said, "Watch me," I realized climbing was a lot more.

A climber can create danger for himself by placing less protection than he should, thus risking a longer fall. But when the crack runs out and you *can't* slot a nut or hammer in a piton, no matter how much you might want and need it, then moxie, intelligence, sportsmanship and confidence enter the game, and climbing becomes much more than a game.

Sandy finally reached the top and, after whacking home a few anchor pins, yelled down that I was on belay and the rope quickly came snug. A horrible, thrashing epic followed. I held the common belief that rock climbing was a bastard son of mountain climbing, and that my boots— gigantic, lug-soled clodhoppers suitable for K2 in winter— were just the article. Not so. They skated all over the walls of the chute and I could never find decent purchase. Hammering the pitons loose was so exhausting I twice had to slouch onto the rope to accomplish it. I smacked my fingers with the hammer, wore two holes in my pants, raked the skin off my shins and fingers and made an egregious ass of myself. But when I finally clawed onto the top of that 100-foot pitch, I knew the taste of success was never so sweet as on the summit of some sheer desert crag that nearly drove me down in despair from the Herculean effort to achieve it. And now it was time to go down.

The image of a climber "roping down" the cliff side, bounding in arcs, meters from the wall, seems to embody everything quixotic in climbing, though there is no climbing involved. I considered myself brave, but when Sandy chucked the rope off and I watched it free-fall 100 feet down the vertical drop, and when Sandy had rigged my

▲▲▲

Rappeling

"Abseil" (European), "rappel" (American), "roping down"—call it what you want, it all involves using friction to descend a rope. The procedure is basic and can be learned in less than an hour. First, you have an anchor. It is easiest to imagine a giant I bolt sunk into the top of the rock. The top of the I bolt forms a circle through which the rope is doubled. Say the rock is 60 feet high. If you were to look at it from below, you would see both ends of the rope on the ground. You could follow one end up, to where it passes through the I bolt, and then comes back down to the ground to the other end. Now picture yourself at the I bolt and the doubled rope. You construct either a "break bar" with carabiners (snaplinks), or using a special device (both rigs must be clipped onto the front of your harness), you feed the doubled rope through the rappeling rig, which in effect crimps the rope via friction, allowing you to descend at a controlled rate of speed, and to stop completely and easily by gripping the rope below the device and/or passing the line over your hip or under a leg. The device does most of the work, while the added friction of holding the rope against your body (often unnecessary) simply controls your speed.

The heroic shots of climbers bounding way off from the cliff side are bogus and dangerous, for speed rappeling heats up the rappel device to the extent that it can singe the sheath of the rope, while the wild bounds put unnecessary stress on the anchor. Once down, the climber unclips from the rope, and simply pulls one end of the doubled rope through the anchor overhead, thus retrieving the rope. The anchor, usually a permanent one, is left behind.

▲

rappel and I inched toward the lip, I knew the second I stepped over the edge I would plunge down the rope and die. That first step over the lip is the longest of anyone's climbing career, and a few people never get past it. But once I slipped onto the vertical wall and felt the security and ease of the system, and the exhilaration of sliding over no-man's-land, I was hooked for life.

Sandy and I climbed several more pitches that day in November 1969, until my hands couldn't take any more no matter how willing my mind was. About twenty years later, I thought I won the Irish Sweepstakes (I didn't), and that's how I felt driving all the way home. Moreover, I understood that there was a sane means of making your way up a cliff that reflected a long history of thought, and that the notion of risking your life to scale a little desert crag was bunk. But it hadn't always been that way.

It wasn't until much later that I could appreciate the decades of trial and error, and the many lives that were sacrificed, in the development of the system and equipment that allowed me to climb a desert cliff in relative safety. It began in the mid-1700s in the European Alps, where certain men aspired to climb the grand peaks surrounding them. The summit was their ultimate goal, and glaciers and snow slopes provided the most natural passage to the top. Following the first recorded Alpine ascent, that of Mt. Aiguille, the rush was on, and major peaks were climbed in succession.

After the easier routes were climbed, subsequent mountaineers found that rock climbing skills were necessary to open up new mountains, and they discovered the lower cliffs and crags provided a perfect training ground. Ropes and rudimentary belaying techniques were introduced around the turn of the twentieth century. In Austria—circa 1910—rappeling was invented, along with heavy steel carabiners and pitons. With the new equipment and techniques, and the confidence they spawned, Austrian and German climbers pushed the standards hard.

Though isolated rock summits were occasionally bagged, the endeavor was considered of "lesser" worth than achieving the big summits of the Alps. In retrospect, some of the "training climbs" on these "practice" cliffs were remarkably difficult, considering that the leaders had little more than hemp ropes (which routinely broke), hemp-soled shoes and boldness to see them through.

Meanwhile, in pre–World War I England, rock climbing on the many backyard outcrops was being explored. The English discouraged the use of pitons, however, partly for ethical reasons, partly owing to the fragile nature of the "gritstone" (soft sandstone). In the absence of big mountains, the English developed crag climbing as a sport in its own right. In the Americas, the sport's development followed the European lead, though roped climbing did not arrive until the late 1920s.

The 1930s heralded the golden age of Alpine climbing, though the focus remained on the major ridges and faces of the higher peaks. During this prewar period, rock climbing standards rose steadily throughout the world, and though most of the glory was still in achieving mountainous summits—Alpine, American and Asian peaks were conquered in succession—in many areas, it was rock climbing standards that saw the most dramatic development.

World War II prompted technological developments that greatly impacted postwar climbing. Before, pitons and carabiners were expensive and rare; ropes were still fashioned from natural fibers, bulky and known to snap on long falls.

"The leader must not fall" was the incontrovertible dictum that all climbers observed if they wanted anything but a brief career. World War II changed all this by providing the plentiful supply of surplus army pitons, lightweight aluminum carabiners, and most important, strong and light nylon ropes.

During the next twenty years, standards rose steadily in both England and the United States. English climbers maintained their antipiton stance and developed anchoring techniques that used runners over natural rock spikes and the wedging of pebbles—and eventually machine nuts slung with slings—as chockstones in cracks. Not surprisingly, the English also pushed standards of boldness. They had little choice, for their protection was dicey writ large. European standards were consolidated but, with their continued emphasis on attaining Alpine summits, actual rock climbing standards advanced little, outside of some exploration of large boulder summits in an area outside Paris. European manufacturers did, however, develop new nylon ropes that were stronger and much easier to handle.

By the early 1960s, specialized rock climbing shoes appeared that were quite similar to what is available today: the Varappe, essentially a tennis shoe upper with a smooth rubber sole. These shoes, from England and France, and the improved design of American pitons, spurred standards upward. In the Americas and England, rock climbing was firmly established as a specialized sport, and routes that led, say, merely to a cliff feature or to rappel points in the middle of blank cliffs were commonly done and respected. Increasingly in England, climbers formulated strong aesthetic distinctions between using pitons and artificial aids to pull up on, and using such anchors solely to protect the climbing of the cliff with hands and feet. This latter practice became known as free climbing. Styles and techniques remained largely provincial, and few climbers traveled widely to sample various climbing areas.

This changed dramatically by 1970, due in large part to the innovative development of rock climbing techniques born in California's Yosemite Valley (during the late fifties and through the sixties), which allowed the ascent of the spectacular cliffs there. To learn the piton aid techniques that enabled these ascents, climbers from around the world traveled to Yosemite. While they learned the American techniques, they also left as a heritage their own different approaches. By the early 1970s, American and English climbers completely dominated the development of the sport, and methods and equipment for climbing rock were becoming homogenized.

Americans pitched the clunkier boots they had generally favored and adopted sensitive French and English smooth-soled shoes; in addition, the destructive and strenuous American pitoning techniques used in scaling the big cliffs were found to be less effective for free climbing than the gentler English nutting techniques. Moreover, innovative Americans started redesigning and commercially producing light and effective protection devices: first, aluminum nuts, then spring-loaded camming units. Simultaneously, rope manufacturers had been fine-tuning and improving their products to achieve the proper balance between strength, energy-absorbing stretch and durability, which led to a much more relaxed attitude toward falling.

By 1980, many climbers were traveling the world to explore different areas, and climbers from many countries were involved in pushing standards. While the best climbers now trained exclusively for climbing (the techniques and equipment were common to all), a new, pure gymnastic approach was applied to the style of ascent, particularly by the French. While this did not change the way that most climbers climbed, it resulted in further fundamental shifts away from the roots of rock climbing as simply one of a number of skills necessary to gain the top of Alpine peaks.

Following my first trip to Joshua Tree, I was a hero with my friends back home. I passed on all that I had learned, and went to the very store Sandy had recommended and bought the very books and manuals Sandy had told me to buy. We devoured these and anything else that had the least bearing on our quest to some day stand atop the world. In school I slipped guidebooks inside my texts and read about the wonders of Yosemite and the High Sierras while everyone else slogged through *Beowulf*.

That was how my days at Upland High passed—tune out the teacher, read a little more about Willie Unsold on Everest, and look up, shifting a little so I could peer out the dirty windows, letting my mind rove, first out 50 feet to a bank of tall conifers that cut the view and blocked off the world, and then pushing further, out past Upland city limits, past Mt. Baldy and into a vertical world I pictured as raw and heroic, liberating. Bold mountaineers in woolen knickers with red socks and green felt alpine hats, hacking up mountains of ice, with hissing forked lightning and hail like buckshot, and a mountain lake, cool and clear as a blue eye staring, ringed by spires and minarets, higher and steeper than I had ever imagined. Beyond the conifers.

But it was all in my mind because I wasn't doing any climbing. None of us could bum a car to get out to Joshua on a consistent basis, even if we did have the gear—which we didn't—or the coin to rent Sandy again. In despair, I called up Sandy and said, "I'm sixteen years old and I work in a gas station. I've got three other buddies who are just as keen as I am but we've got no car, no gear and almost no money. What gives, Sandy?"

Sandy steered us to the Rock Climbing Section (RCS) of the Sierra Club, and we enrolled in the beginning climbing course, which met twice a week at the local junior college. The RCS class was an odd mix of dottering old duffers, Eagle Scouts and hippies, and we fit into that group like Swedes in Chad. Following three weeks of wearisome lectures and written examinations, we began belay tests, catching a 100-pound pail of cement dropped from so high that arresting it nearly cut smaller students in half. Several times the rope got away from people and they staggered off with nasty rope burns about their backsides. We coiled ropes, hundreds of ropes hundreds of times, but we didn't go climbing. We fingered pitons and carabiners and learned to tie our knots with one hand and in the shower and in the dark. But we didn't go climbing. We saw slide shows and movies and went over the climbing signals so many times I could recite them all backward. And finally, after eleven weeks, we went climbing.

Mt. Rubidoux, in Riverside, California, is not a mountain at all, just a swollen knoll a couple miles square and about 300 feet high, with a towering white cross on the summit. It is covered with big brown boulders, and has been a popular practice climbing area for decades. That first RCS outing to Rubidoux reflected a trend that I would see throughout my climbing career—that many "climbers" consider a trip to the crags a social event, to be performed in great numbers, to involve all manner of yakking and gear shuffling and cocking about, but hardly any climbing. We lugged enormous coolers of punch and ice water, enough gear to siege Makalu and vittles sufficient to cross

Sumatra on foot. There were speeches and orientation lectures from fat gaffers in lederhosen and glacier goggles, who stopped often for effect, or to answer silly questions—and they kept on for hours. Like many outdoor "educators," their pride in talking was matched only by our boredom in listening. Finally we broke for lunch. At about three that afternoon, we split into groups of twenty-five, and around sundown, I got a chance to "climb" a 15-foot slab.

By then, my personal climbing club was reduced to Rick Accomazzo, who would later go on to become an All-American water polo player and one of the country's great face climbers, and myself, still a hard-core baseball player. We noticed that most every boulder had a permanent bolt anchor on top, that it was a quick and easy business to rig a toprope—where the rope runs from the ground, up and through an anchor on top of the rock, and back down to the ground—and have hundreds of climbs at the ready. I asked Ricky if he thought we really needed fifty-five gallons of Kool-Aid, eight dozen deli sandwiches and a lot of talk about gear and where to take a leak. "No," he said, "We need a rope." We jumped into his mom's Pinto and raced home.

I got the three ten-dollar bills I had stashed in the pages of Herzog's *Annapurna* and Ricky came up with the same. We went to the Backpacker Shop, bought our first rope, three slings and six carabiners, and drove straight back to Rubidoux the next morning. It would be the first of a thousand such trips.

We'd string a rope and climb till our fingers wouldn't have it any more. On one of our first trips to Rubidoux, we met Richard Harrison, who was from our high school, though he had so little use for Upland High he'd recently

▲▲▲

The Rope

The rope is the lifeline, the primary piece of equipment to any climber. There is not a single serious climber whose life has not been saved by the rope, so obviously ropes are extremely reliable. Since 1945, all viable climbing ropes have been fashioned from nylon, composed of a woven nylon sheath over a braided core. Though there are isolated cases of ropes being cut over sharp edges or chopped by rockfall, a modern climbing rope has never simply broken from the impact of a fall. There is so much overkill built into the system that a rope in good condition has no chance of breaking whatsoever, no matter how severe a fall it withstands. A certain amount of stretch is built into the lines to ease the jolt of any lengthy fall. Standard dimensions are 50 meters (165 feet) in length, and 10 to 11 millimeters in diameter. Most weigh about 8 to 9 pounds, cost in the neighborhood of $150 dollars and are good for several seasons.

▲

quit—to devote his life to climbing. And so began a partnership that would last to this writing. Many nights found us three huddled in the basement below Richard's mother's house, which was covered with posters of the late, great Willie Unsold on the West Ridge of Everest, the French on K2 and a tall, smashing Nubian with a scarlet turban on her billowing bouffant. (She had nothing to do with climbing, but hers was the best poster.) The next day, we were always back at the boulders.

The climbing at Rubidoux was essentially "bouldering," climbing on rocks small enough so that a rope is usually unnecessary. The world's hardest climbing—in terms of individual moves and small sequences—has always been, and always will be, on the boulders. The controlled medium, the ease of trying, trying and trying again, and the ferocious, though normally friendly, competition that surrounds the pastime are ideal conditions for the best climbers to try the hardest sequences imaginable.

Early on, Richard, Ricky and I learned that bouldering was the quickest way to gain climbing skill, and for three months, we virtually lived at Rubidoux, scraping up the problems, learning to relax and focus, getting our bodies accustomed to "cranking." As Sandy had promised, a journeyman's grasp of ropework came quickly. Not so the actual climbing. Few sports are more physical, and none can so demolish the fingers and forearms. Until the finger pads get calloused, latching dime-sized crystals and edges feels like clasping broken glass. The finger joints, bent double on a hard pull, ache horribly until they're accustomed to the stress. And the back and calves must grow very strong. During those first few months, I'd often return home with my "tips" so lacerated I couldn't hold a pencil, my forearms so pumped I couldn't make a fist. But it was a sweet pain, for we were getting better, quickly.

Then we met Phil Haney. Only when you have seen technique performed imperfectly can you appreciate a wizard, and when we saw Haney climb, we immediately knew we were watching one. Perhaps five foot ten, he had a torso like a scaled-down Hermes, shoulder-length red hair and a face off one of those flyers in the post office—but maybe that's because his eyes were so focused. His gear consisted of gym shorts, Varappe boots and a chalk bag. We first caught him working out on the "Joe Brown" boulder, a 50-foot, featureless wall that overhung about 120 degrees for the first 20 feet. We'd never seen anybody climb it, and never thought anyone could. So we were amazed as Haney latched imperceptible holds and literally launched himself skyward, slapping for and snagging the merest wrinkle or divot, the last millimeter of his skintight boots toeing rounded nothings. He'd hang from one arm and casually dip his free hand into a small chalk bag at his waist, his eyes playing over the impossible rock above him. Then he'd coil up and vault off, fluid, precise, controlled. Inside of fifteen minutes, Haney had scaled that face six times by six different routes. We couldn't have been more amazed had we seen a dairy cow long jump the Grand Canyon. Those fifteen minutes watching Phil Haney changed our lives.

It is interesting to remember the time when we were finally good enough to repeat Haney's performance. Once we'd climbed those routes, we knew that Haney was world class—or had been—yet he was virtually unknown in the climbing world. The reason, though rare, was not unheard of. For some climbers, a long fall, like a bad rap or memories of love, will follow them everywhere and always. I later learned that Haney had taken such a fall. Though he'd walked away unscathed, that 50-foot ripper had taken all his nerve, and his imagination, running away with what *might* have happened, kept him from ever getting it back. He never climbed anything bigger than a 50-foot boulder again, so far as I know.

Haney's remarkable exhibition reoriented us instantly and completely. We asked him about the Varappe boots, which we'd never seen and which resembled tight, high-top sneakers with a smooth rubber sole. They were European imports made specifically for "rock gymnastics," as he called it. And the chalk bag? "For the grip." We drove home, put our lug-soled mountaineering boots in the garage, folded up our knickers, drove into Los Angeles and bought Varappe boots and chalk bags. In two days, we were back at Rubidoux dressed exactly like Phil Haney.

It would be an age before we could climb like Haney, but the new Varappes allowed us to stand on holds unthinkable in clunky mountaineering boots, and the chalk greatly improved our grip. What helped the most, however, was our new thinking: that rock climbing was a sport, a form of gymnastics. We still drew our inspiration from mountain climbing books—as far as wanting to bag the big peak in a flourish of grit and valor—but our strategy was different. We'd tackle the big peak in time, but we'd show up in gym trunks and skin tight rock slippers, hands dusted with chalk. First, though, we'd have to tackle the small peak, which we could finally do, since Ricky now had a car.

It was summertime, and temperatures out at Joshua Tree were in the hundreds, so our first trip to a genuine cliff was to Tahquitz and Suicide rocks in Idyllwild, California. After three months buffing technique and ropework at Rubidoux, we were anxious to see how we'd fare on the crag where America's pioneer rock climbers had been having at it since as early as 1936, establishing some of the country's most historic routes.

I will never forget my first view of Tahquitz. After 20 miles of steep mountain driving, we rounded a bend and there it was—marble white and magnificent, rearing off the escarpment 10 miles across Strawberry Valley. Perhaps a lot of the splendor of climbing is overstated, but no sport is performed on a more dazzling venue. Like all great monoliths, Tahquitz is nature's magnum opus, and it makes you feel bad to know that someday you will die and never see it again. And just seeing it was quite enough that first time. We immediately decided to go across the valley to Suicide Rock, which, at 300 feet, looked casual in comparison.

By the time we had hiked up to the base of Suicide, which now towered above us like a solemn gray vault, it didn't look so informal a proposition. We thumbed through the guidebook and decided on a route called "Frustration," rated at 5.10.

A guidebook, a veritable road map for cliff travelers, lists and details first ascents—from the names and dates of the first people to climb a given route, to the location of the anchors and any other pertinent information. Each route is named and rated by the first ascentionists and, by the time a route makes it into print, it's usually had enough ascents that the rating is fairly objective, arrived at by consensus. I don't know why the hell we picked Frustration for our first route at Suicide, but it certainly lived up to its name.

If a climb or a rock is popular with climbers, it will always have a name: Rixon's Pinnacle, Elephant Rock, Geek Towers, Paisano Pinnacle, to name a few. The names come from all sorts of sources. Some say Elephant Rock resembles an elephant when looked at just the right way. Paisano Pinnacle won its name from the gallon of wine Mark Powell guzzled on the summit after making the first ascent. I later learned that Frustration had driven the first ascent party half mad trying to reckon how to climb it. Sometimes the names are purely arbitrary. The real value is that the name stick, so climbers know what and where the routes are.

Anyway, the danger of those first few months is that you *don't know* exactly what you're doing—you don't know if the anchor is bombproof, if your knots are secure, if you're keeping to the route, if you're climbing yourself into that irreversible jam where any move will bring disaster that much closer. You believe you know, or you hope you know, but you wouldn't bet your life on it. Yet that is exactly what you feel you're doing. In time, usually after a handful of climbs, you will know; but trembling up those first few climbs always seems like snatching cheese from a set mousetrap. Nowadays, you always serve a brief apprenticeship under someone who does know—usually a guide—and you, in turn, learn quickly. But we could barely come up with gas money, to say nothing of paying for a guide, so it was just us and the cheese.

The blunderings and methods we used that first day were exactly the same as those used by any other gung ho team on their initial climb. Naturally, Frustration was far too hard a route for us. Ricky led off with alacrity, but he slowed and wobbled and turned cadaverous at the first difficulties. As he clawed to a roof about 30 feet up, Richard and I started the standard ritual that always ensures a team of experiencing two climbs at once—the one you see, and the one you hear. Ricky was shaking like he had dengue fever, but safe on the deck, we were yelling, "Looking solid, Ricky." "Almost got that jug." "Another foot." "Yeah. Go for it." "You're making it look *easy*."

All of these were shameless lies, screamed in the hope of rallying Ricky straight to the summit so we wouldn't have to take the frightening lead. Then, a toe popped or a hand slipped, and Ricky fell about 10 inches onto the top piton. We lowered him to the ground and helped him untie the knot, because he was too pumped to untie it himself. I was sweating the big drop because it was my turn. I scratched up to the roof and had no sooner noticed the big knob about 50 feet above when the shameless chorus chimed in: "Almost got the knob, John baby." "Lookin' solid. Another foot." "It's all yours." "You own it." I fell off. They lowered me back down and I collapsed, sucking down half the sky in panicked mouthfuls.

This is not the normal way to go about it, but is the only way if you're in a hurry to get good. Most climbers enter the sport for the same reasons people go hiking or mountain biking or river running—to break the rote of everyday living, to get outdoors where you can crack a sweat and grab a manageable thrill amongst company similarly disposed. Purged by fear, even moderate climbing requires such focus that hassles and heartaches are left on the deck below, growing smaller and smaller as you mount on. Logging numerous falls, shaking with terror and goading your partners to meet their Maker is foolishness at its worst and most dangerous. But we wouldn't have wanted it any other way.

By about mid-afternoon, Ricky, Richard and I had sieged our way about 70 feet up the first pitch of Frustration. In the process, another inviolate rule naturally evolved: The leader could never come down simply because he didn't "like the looks of things." He could only get lowered to the ground once he'd *proved* he could not do it—i.e., he'd fallen off. Certainly you could show fear (and would)—for legs to wobble and hands to twitch and to "sweat like pork"—but you could never admit it. When the leader would claw up another few feet, whack in a piton and slump back exhausted, whoever was next in line *had* to assume the lead. Most likely, he had not recovered from his last assault. So you'd humor him and lie to him, fetch him the canteen, gum, food if you had any. You'd try everything but an iron lung to bring your man around but by God or without Him, he was going next because it was *his turn*.

After another hour of swapping turns—which won us about 20 new feet—we were confounded, especially by Frustration's 5.10 rating. Free-climbing ratings then ran from 5.0 to 5.11. The 5 was for fifth class, which covered free climbing; so a 5.10 was a fifth-class climb to the tenth degree. We couldn't then imagine what heroics a 5.11 route would entail. Richard suggested we'd need plumber's helpers for hands.

▲▲▲
Rating the Difficulty

The decimal rating system is a climber's only yardstick as to how difficult a given climb is, and for this reason, it is both simple and comprehensive. The American rating system that follows is one of many in use around the world.

CLASS

1. *Walking.*
2. *Hiking.* Mostly on established trails, or perhaps slogging along a stream bed.
3. *Scrambling.* Angle is steep enough where hands are used for balance. A handline is rarely used, even by inexperienced climbers.
4. *Climbing risky enough that a fall could be fatal.* Pulling with your arms required. A rope, some equipment and protection techniques are used by most mountaineers.
5. *Technical rock climbing, commonly called free climbing.* A rope, specialized equipment and techniques are always used to protect against a fall. Fifth-class climbing is the subject of *How to Rock Climb!*
6. *Rock so sheer or holdless that ascent by using hands and feet is impossible.* The equipment is used directly to aid the ascent, hence the common usage names for class-six climbing: artificial, direct aid or, simply, aid climbing. Recall the hoary image of the intrepid climber hammering his way up the rock, his weight suspended on a succession of creaky pins. This image still best illustrates what aid climbing is all about.

It is commonly agreed that technical rock climbing starts at fifth class. Fifth-class climbing varies from low-angle slabs, where only the beginner will relish a rope, to 125-degree face climbs so extreme that world-class climbers might fall fifty times before they work out the entire sequence, if indeed they ever do. The "decimal" system is an open-ended system that now includes climbs from 5.0, the easiest, to 5.14+, to date the most difficult leads achieved. Climbs of 5.10 through 5.14 are in the realm of the advanced or expert climber; to better shade the nuances of these advanced levels, the letters a, b, c and d were tacked onto the rating. For example, 5.12d represents the extreme end of the 5.12 standard, whereas a 5.12a or 5.12b is an easier, low-end 5.12.

Anyway, with about an hour of daylight left, Richard finally grappled onto the big ledge atop the first pitch of Frustration, anchored off to a big pine tree and retched. We'd exchanged the lead no less than twenty times between us, each attack getting us one piton and a few precious feet closer to home. Of course, the main difficulties were not technical, rather psychological. None of us could get more than about three feet above a piton without freezing in terror. But once we had the impunity of the toprope, where slack is taken in as you climb and a fall means nothing but slipping back onto a semitaut line, Ricky and I dashed up the pitch in a heartbeat. We watched the sun go down from the ledge, and rappeled off in the dark, thinking nothing of it because our many trips to Rubidoux had gotten us past our fears of rappeling. Naturally, the rope got hung up when we tried to pull it back down after the rappel, and it was midnight before we got it free.

* * *

Climbing quickly turns into a debacle when facing difficult routes without sufficient knowledge, experience and conditioning to handle them. But our debacle on Frustration was more the outcome of our fright at finally finding ourselves out on the lead, and looking at genuine falls—however harmless—rather than shortcomings in our actual ability. As is always the case with beginning leaders, we needed courage. But sane courage—the only kind that keeps you healthy—comes with the confidence that comes from experience, and there is simply no way to shortcut the process. There are, however, ways to hasten it.

The accepted method is to start with the "trade routes," the easy, well-traveled climbs that everyone breaks in on. Slowly, prudently—perhaps over a couple of seasons—you work your way up to the harder climbs. So goes the standard thinking. But we were too antsy to wait two years or even two months, so we developed another strategy. If we could somehow hone our climbing techniques to the sharpest edge, we reasoned, then moves on the actual routes would seem easy—or at least doable—and the horror of leading them would be that much less. It was a peculiar approach, but a practical one, since we could get out to Rubidoux almost every day. Plus, Richard had found another bouldering area in the mountains behind his house, with steeper, smoother and more difficult problems than those at Rubidoux.

So we set the gear aside for a time, and hit the boulders with a vengeance. And we started cross-training as well, doing countless fingertip pull-ups in Richard's basement, lifting weights, running and doing withering laps through an obstacle course at the local college. Slowly, we started getting "honed." Our muscles quit aching, and unlike before, we no longer burned out after a couple hours of bouldering. We'd spend entire days taunting each other to crank harder, step higher, to forget the raw, sometimes bleeding fingertips and "flash it." If one of us mastered a difficult problem, it was only a matter of days, or minutes, before the others did it as well.

It is strangely fantastic to reflect back to these early days, when all our dreams were open-ended and unfulfilled. Not so many years have passed, but life is measured by the potholes, not the length of the road. A person has but one chance in life, when he is young and foolish and ignorant, to absolutely and perfectly desire something as I then desired to get onto the high crag. It's the genius of not knowing the "proper" proportion of things, of focusing everything on what you wanted, not what others thought you needed. The best part of it all is how clean and honest it all felt, following desire so precisely, with no pathos or pretense or second thoughts at all. It seemed that if we didn't follow our calling, all was lost, and life would never make any sense to us. Only later would things get too complex and muddled to think and act so decisively, and only later would I realize that those early days on the boulders were the best days after all.

Every exacting physical discipline has its own skills, and these must be mindfully performed time and time again to have any chance at mastery. And since no two climbs or even set of holds are the same, climbing is an ever-changing problem-solving design.

When facing a plane, arête or dihedral of rock, an erect body can assume only so many postures. The nuances are endless, but the generic forms are finite. The continuum of moves, the actual sequences, vary from one climb to another, even with uniform cracks. Whatever the configuration, you can only execute one move at a time. So the real

▲▲▲

Training

Twenty years ago, only the rare fellow trained specifically for climbing. Certainly, mountaineers made sure they were "fit" before heading to the Himalayas, but most rock climbers simply went cragging to get in shape. In many circles, cross-training was considered nonsense. And those who did train often went about things incorrectly. Back then, the focus was on one-arm pull-ups, fingertip chin-ups, and a host of other drills that resulted in more injuries than strong climbers. While there is still no definitive workout regime for rock climbers, weight training has caught on. Also, various manufacturers have produced a slew of "hangboards," cast-resin boards featuring differing widths of surfaces on which to do pull-ups. Perhaps the most important cross-training device has been the advent of indoor climbing gyms—walls up to 60 feet high fitted with synthetic handholds to simulate a crag. These have started to spring up all over the country, and are particularly popular as training grounds for college physical-education classes. No matter what the future holds, the basic, in-home exercise will always remain the pull-up bar set between doorjambs.

▲

value of bouldering is that if you do enough of it, you build up a library of moves, recognizing what works where, while schooling yourself on the appropriate response. Hoping to become a great free climber without the foundation of bouldering is like trying to become a penetrating fiction writer without ever reading a novel. Given a background in bouldering, a leader never approaches a climb cold since whatever the required moves and sequences prove to be, you've no doubt seen and probably done similar ones on the boulders. And so the more experience a climber gets, the more the game becomes a matter of mind. Can you recognize the moves? Can you select the right sequence? And can you execute it? Are you prepared for the consequences if you cannot? One of the enduring draws of climbing is that the deeper you delve into its mysteries, the deeper you delve into your own mind.

During those formative months bouldering at Rubidoux and Mt. Baldy, we naturally returned to favorite problems, and over time, developed a circuit. As the weeks passed, more difficult problems were added until there wasn't much at either Rubidoux or Baldy that we couldn't do; and there were more than a few problems that only we could do. The time had come to hit the high crag again. We went back to Suicide and I led the first pitch of Frustration in about five minutes. Richard, Ricky and I had arrived.

It is interesting to note that as our technical skills rose, so rose our appreciation for the whole endeavor; and there is nothing grander in a climber's life than to finally become a genuine leader. Most veterans agree that climbing doesn't really start until you cast off on the lead. You can boulder around enchanted forests and follow a leader up the world's greatest climbs, but the moment you're first on the rope— out on the "sharp end"—it's suddenly real in a different way. Everything is magnified, because now you're playing for keeps. The decisions are all yours, as are the rewards and consequences. Whether that first lead is up a route like Frustration, or on some filthy slab in a scrap-heap quarry, the feeling of command and the special demands are always the same. It's no longer just an exhilarating physical challenge, but a creative problem-solving design requiring a lot of intangible things and having the penalty of injury or even death for a major oversight.

To remain calm and never panic in the face of a fall are things a beginning leader can rarely manage; but an experienced one usually can. Therein lies the nobility of a really ace leader—the knack to carry on under duress. Leading is a milieu where illusions are few and sham reputations short-lived, and it takes a special kind of mind to dominate the cliff with grace and confidence. The nature of a risk taker's mind is a topic of endless discussion and few answers. I've found that climbers tend to be restless and physical, and need a struggle to avoid feeling temporary about themselves. I've also found that many are hounded by boredom, and in radical cases, only on the edge can they make their lives possible at all. Though people's needs and reasons are unique, most climbers find that out on the lead they feel more alive than anywhere else.

The Southern California rock climbing scene had for decades revolved around Tahquitz and Suicide rocks. During the fifties and early sixties, Royal Robbins, Tom Frost, Yvon Chouinard, TM Herbert, Mark Powell, Bob Kamps—those who thrust American climbing ahead of the rest of the world with their exploits in Yosemite—all broke in at Tahquitz. Later, a second wave swept through Idyllwild led by Lee Harrel, Pat Callis, Charlie Raymond, Tom Higgins and Bud "Ivan" Couch. As fate would have it, that last wave crested out concurrently with the invasion of my generation. As Ricky, Richard and I began making weekly trips to Idyllwild, we met and befriended other young climbers who maintained the same agenda—to blow away the existing standards and establish our own. Rob Muir of Riverside and Mike Graham of Newport Beach were the first young Turks we met.

Rob was a distant relative of John Muir, historic sage of the woods and patriarch of the American parks system. Rob came from Berkeley, and brought a little of that city's funk with him, including a Davy Crockett ponytail and a yen for macrobiotic rations. He was skinny as a rake, but with his wonderfully educated fingers he could pull on razor-thin holds as if they were guardrails. Mike was a prodigy, with limited drive and unlimited talent. He so quickly mastered technique that the art seemed invented just for him. Once he had a hold of the basics, he skipped all apprenticeship and jumped straight into worldclass. Within a few weekends, we became interchangeable partners. Our itinerary was just this: Climb all of the hardest routes in the shortest possible time. We all were talented on the boulders, but had little leading experience—a condition that didn't last long.

For all climbers, the process of becoming a skilled, confident leader is exhilarating because everything is new. Most of the climbs at Suicide ascend steep faces, bereft of cracks and ledges. Once you worked your way some hundreds of feet up one of these spectacular walls, following holds sometimes so minuscule you had to squint to find them, feelings of freedom and sometimes fear could overwhelm you. And those first hanging belays were unbelievable.

Since there often were no ledges to anchor and belay from, many pitches ended nowhere at all. The belay was marked only by two tiny bolts bristling from a blank wall, drilled and driven home by the first-ascent party. (Modern bolts are normally ⅜ inches by 1¼ inches, and have a sheer strength exceeding 3,000 pounds. Most versions feature an expandable sleeve/shank that keeps them secure in the hole for decades. Unreliable bolts, though not unheard of, are rare. In any event, climbers usually have to trust them.) You would tie yourself off taut to the bolts, then clip off and sit back in a belay seat, more commonly called a "butt bag." In design, it resembled a bosun's chair, except the rope was a loop of nylon sling and the seat consisted of a dinky patch of rip-stop nylon sewn to the looped sling. Your first experience dangling in one of these is about as soothing as sitting in the electric chair, but the butt bag shifts a lot more. Yet you quickly come to relish these hanging belays, dangling in open space, gazing over the low green fan of trees, you and your partner clinging dots on a convex wall, like gnats on a great rotunda. Sometimes I'd filch a couple of my dad's cigars to stoke and enjoy, hanging in my butt bag, the whole world spread out below me. We were seventeen. We would never die.

As we got better and more experienced, our group grew that much tighter. Within a couple of months, we had climbed many of the hardest routes at Suicide and Tahquitz, which were widely held to be among the hardest face climbs in the country. Our weekday workouts in Richard's basement and bouldering sessions at Rubidoux and Baldy grew more intense. Yet as our experience grew, so did our respect for the climbers who had established the routes we were checking off. When you're just getting started, you think you're blazing a trail. Then one day, dangling in your butt bag, you glance down and notice the beaten track. But one track was not beaten. In fact, it had only been climbed once. That route, called "Valhalla," was the hardest climb at either Tahquitz or Suicide, and was then one of the few routes in the world to bear a 5.11 rating.

Scraping and battling on, our focus turned to Valhalla for several reasons. Climbing a 5.11 route was a dream. But there also was the thorny issue of Bud "Ivan" Couch, who had made the first ascent of Valhalla. A flinty, unsentimental man, Bud was de facto lord of Suicide and Tahquitz, had established many of the hardest climbs, and was the sole active survivor of the previous era. Perhaps ten years older than we, he seemed to stand about seven feet tall, was a professor of some abstruse science and had watched us from the start—had seen the many long falls, had heard our whimpering, had at times watched us climb with such exaggerated concern that it was indistinguishable from cowardice. He'd also seen us attack the crags with all the subtlety of a jackhammer, and he categorically scorned us as punks, hacks and zealots.

Only the greatest climbers give their peers time to think that way about them, and despite his stony handling of us, we all considered Bud one of the great ones, an artist and a pioneer. His technique was burnished gold; ours was pot iron. Yet we were making it up many of his tougher climbs, not gracefully, but on gumption and fire, and the limelight was panning our way. Bud was confounded that we of so little talent and experience should get so far. When it became common knowledge that we were taking a bead on the hallowed Valhalla—often tried, but as yet unrepeated—Bud showed his teeth. If we so much as dreamed about climbing Valhalla, we'd have to wake up and apologize. The gauntlet was thus thrown down: If Bud wouldn't hand over the standard, we'd rip it from his hands. When after another month we all had climbed Valhalla, some of us a dozen times, Bud was astonished, and saw himself elbowed out of the opera house by kids who could merely scream.

Our ascent of Valhalla was the most significant, and by far the most marvelous, thing I had ever done in my life. In looking back I recall how poor a student I was, how I struggled to get along with my folks, was ornery, anxious, bitter for reasons I couldn't then fathom, and how I carried around with me all the insecurities that accompany a young man who thinks he's no good and will never accomplish anything worth a damn. But climbing Valhalla had transformed that self-image in one bold stroke. For days afterwards, I walked around with quicksand under my feet, and would sometimes wake up in the still of the night, get up and walk outside and yell "I climbed Valhalla!" There is something mildly psychotic about all of this, and the same can be said about the whole business.

Anyway, after we'd mastered Valhalla the standard was ours, and soon our little group took on the aspect of a proper club. We called ourselves "The Stonemasters." There were no dues, no meetings, no secret handshakes. Initiation was automatic to anyone who led Valhalla. Years later, much would be written about The Stonemasters, mostly outright lies, or stories so lavishly embellished that they amounted to the same thing. Forming The Stonemasters was a statement that we had arrived, and would take no prisoners.

For us, climbing had grown into a sort of all-consuming passion. A vice. Balzac said it costs as much to support a family as it does a vice. If that's true, said family would have scraped by living out of trash cans. Like most who had set out to vanquish the climbing world, we were so busted we found it hard enough to keep Ricky's Pinto running. But we kept it on the road through the winter and fall, when the standards at Suicide and Tahquitz rocks changed forever.

All of The Stonemasters added some special nostrum to the group, but nobody furnished such energy, drive and raw entertainment as did Tobin Sorrenson. He was the most conspicuous proponent of a madman to ever lace up Varappes. Climbing had never seen the likes of Tobin, and probably never will again. The exploits of his short life deserve a book. Two books.

The first time we met, or rather saw, Tobin, Richard, Ricky and I were, ironically, walking beneath Valhalla. The air was shattered by a ghastly scream, and we glanced up to see a body cartwheeling down, arms flailing. The rope finally stopped him, jerking Tobin right side up and slamming him into the wall with a dull thump. He hung limp for a moment, twitching. Then he shook it off and in his inimitable boyish voice said, "Biscuit. I almost had it." Throughout the following winter, Tobin would almost "have it" untold times, then would pitch off for spectacular falls that should have ended his career, and his life, ten times over. Yet he'd always shake it off and claw straight back onto the route for another go. And usually got it.

He had the body of a welterweight, a lick of sandy brown hair and the faraway gaze of the born maniac; yet he had a buoyancy about him that survived all the horror, and carried on with the precocity and innocence of a child. He would never cuss, or show the slightest hostility, and around girls he was so shy he'd flush and stammer. But out on the sharp end of the rope he was a fiend in human form. Most climbers loved to work out on safe, practice routes, committing to the scary and demanding leads only on occasion and when everything was right. Tobin couldn't be bothered to cock around on any practice routes, and would go only for the hardest, most harrowing climbs even when *nothing* was right.

It's disgraceful if a climber courts danger through ignorance, by flouting all the accepted rules, or through base adventurism. The whole game is about mastery, about that enchanted knack to calculate just how far you can push things and still walk away unmarked. But Tobin, so long as he eventually made his way up the route, didn't give a damn about the closeness of the shave, or what you thought of his methods. He became a world-class climber very quickly, because anyone that well formed and savagely motivated will gain the top in no time—if he doesn't kill himself first. Still, when we started bagging new routes and first free ascents, Tobin continued defying the gods with his electrifying peelers.

The musician who plays purely for recreation, or to beguile his hours away, is perfectly satisfied to play other folks' music, to memorize and even master a favorite solo, perhaps adding a few riffs of his own. But that's all we can presume from him because his craft is, after all, just a hobby, a diversion. But to the player whose life and identity are bound to his instrument, and whose friends are the same, the need to start blowing his own tune comes soon enough. And so we were, anxious to find our own way, to climb our own routes. We'd wrested the standard from Bud Couch and didn't want moss growing on it. So our little band of Stonemasters started nosing around for new things to do.

In rock climbing, "new" climbs can take two forms: the first free ascent, which is actually a new way of climbing an old route; or the first ascent, which is to establish a completely original climb. Both are ambitious statements, and both have their own charm and rewards.

As mentioned, when a first-ascent party cannot climb a new route using hands and feet on available holds (free climbing), direct aid from pitons, nuts, bolts, even skyhooks comes into play. The leader constructs a string of protection, closely spaced, with nylon stirrups clipped to each successive piece; these "aid slings" take the body weight instead of arms and feet. You set a nut or piton, clip in the rope and then the slings, climb up the rung, set another piece above and so on. "Aid," or artificial climbing, as it's also called, is a mechanical occupation, and is as casual or horrendous as the chain of protection is secure or dicey.

If, for instance, the route follows a perfect crack, where each piton is stout enough to anchor a battleship, then the climbing is usually simple, secure and straightforward. Each piece of protection, the individual pitons or nuts and so forth, are "bomb-proof." If the route should follow, say, a flaky, incipient crack bisecting an overhanging wall, however, the protection (some specialty pitons are no bigger than a postage stamp) may support little more than body weight, much less the impact of a fall. When a leader finds himself 100 feet out on a string of creaky placements, regretting that his parents ever met, he steps gingerly indeed from one piece to the next. If the piece he's standing on pops, the pieces in the chain below him will fire from the crack like cloves from a holiday ham, all the way back to the belay anchor.

When climbers first went to Tahquitz, around 1930, they scaled the easiest, most obvious "lines," striking features like chimney or crack systems running from bottom to summit. As later climbers entered the scene, they too wanted to pioneer new routes, and in a few short decades, most all of the outstanding natural routes were bagged. Ensuing climbers, urged by the pioneering spirit, then moved to the more nebulous, sometimes overhanging lines. (It's the same scenario in business: The first guys in town snatch up the easy buck. The next group starts working the fringe for change.) Finding the rock too sheer or blank to free climb, they often "nailed," or aid climbed it. By 1950, most natural lines, however obscure, had been scaled. The only option left for the following climbers was either to tackle the bald faces between cracks (to print their own money), or to try to free climb existing aid routes (to grab someone else's). In 1946, when Chuck Wilts made the first free ascent of the "Piton Pooper," an exceedingly steep line at Tahquitz, he started a trend that would obsess free climbing specialists right up to this writing: to free climb what the other man had to hammer his way up, converting a mechanical exercise into a gymnastic one.

Shortly after The Stonemasters were formed, we began establishing new routes—generally short face climbs at Suicide. But the most stupendous climbs in Idyllwild, both in grandeur of line and reputation, were the big artificial routes at Tahquitz. The problem was that every route thought to be even remotely possible had long been free climbed by the previous generation.

Free climbing those few remaining aid routes would require not only new technique, but new thinking. I'm not sure that our eventual success really came from new thinking, though. It was just that these last aid climbs were the only thing left for us, and our minds were not checked by old notions of what was impossible. They say it takes a fool to conquer the impossible, but maybe he's the only one who tries. Looking back, I realize that much of the trick was purely psychological. These climbs *looked* impossible. The flake was considered too thin, the roof too wide, the face too steep; and believing it so, no one had ever tried to free climb them.

Many of these routes were first climbed by Royal Robbins, Yvon Chouinard, Tom Frost—the biggest legends in American climbing—and free climbing them proved a tremendous confidence booster. Most of us had come from nowhere in particular, and had done nothing more notable than work in a gas station or chase down a fly ball. But in

terms of Tahquitz and Suicide, these ascents were monumental—and we knew it. Climbing was joined to the past
like a piton to a rope, and we were now a little link in the
grand continuum. But not all had gone smoothly. Our failed
attempt to free the "Green Arch" comes to mind.

All through that spring we'd drive up to Idyllwild early
on Saturday mornings, gather in a greasy spoon in the
small village and discuss an itinerary. The air was charged
because we were on a roll, our faith and gusto growing with
each new route. Climbing was rapidly gaining popularity,
and there was talk within the crowd that The Stonemasters
were crazy, or liars or both; and this sat well with us.
Tahquitz was our oyster. We'd pried it open with a piton
and for months had gorged at will; but the fare was running
thin. Since we had ticked off one after another of the old
aid routes, our options had dwindled to only the most grim
or preposterous ones. But, during the previous week, Ricky
Accomazzo had scoped out the Green Arch, an elegant arc
on Tahquitz's southern shoulder. When Ricky mentioned
he thought we just might be capable of free climbing this
pearl of an aid climb, Tobin looked as though the Hound of
the Baskervilles had just heard the word *bone*, and we
nearly had to lash him to the booth so we could finish our
oatmeal.

Since the Green Arch was Ricky's idea, he got the first go
at it. Tobin balked, so we tied him off to a stunted pine and
Ricky started up. After 50 feet of dicey wall climbing, he
gained the arch, which soared above for another 80 feet
before curving right and disappearing in a field of big knobs
and pockets. If we could only get to those knobs, the remaining 300 feet would go easily and the Green Arch would
fall. But the lower corner and the arch above looked bleak.
The crack in the back of the arch was too thin to accept

even fingertips, and both sides of the corner were blank and marble-smooth. By pasting half his rump on one side of the puny corner, and splaying his feet out on the opposite side, Ricky stuck to the rock—barely—both his ass and his boots steadily oozing off the steep, greasy wall. It was exhausting duty just staying put, and moving up was accomplished by a grueling, precarious sequence of quarter-inch moves. Amazingly, Ricky jackknifed about halfway up the arch before his calves pumped out. He lowered off a bunk piton and I took a shot.

After an hour of the hardest climbing I'd ever done, I reached a rest hold just below the point where the arch swept out right and melted into that field of knobs. Twenty feet to pay dirt. But those 20 feet didn't look promising.

There were some sucker knobs just above the arch, but those ran out after about 25 feet and would leave a climber in the bleakest no-man's-land, with nowhere to go, no chance to climb back right onto the route, no chance to get any protection and no chance to retreat. We'd have to stick to the arch.

Finally, I underclung about 10 feet out the arch, whacked in a suspect knife-blade piton, clipped the rope in—and fell off. I lowered to the ground, slumped back, and didn't rise for ten minutes. I had weeping strawberries on both ass cheeks, and my ankles were rubbery and tweaked from splaying them out on the far wall.

Tobin, unchained from the pine, tied into the lead rope and stormed up the corner like a man fleeing Satan on foot. He battled up to the rest hold, drew a few quick breaths, underclung out to that creaky, buckled, driven-straight-up-into-an-expanding-flake knifeblade, and immediately cranked himself over the arch and started heaving up the line of sucker knobs.

"No!" I screamed up. "Those knobs don't go any-where." But it was too late.

Understand that Tobin was a born-again Christian, that he'd smuggled Bibles into Bulgaria risking twenty-five years on a Balkan rock pile, that he'd studied God at a funda-mentalist university, and none of this altered the indisput-able fact that he was perfectly mad. Out on the sharp end, he not only ignored all consequences but actually loathed them, doing all kinds of crazy, incomprehensible things to mock them. (The following year, out at Joshua Tree, Tobin followed a difficult, overhanging crack with a rope noosed around his neck.) Most horrifying was his disastrous ca-pacity to simply charge at a climb pell-mell. On straight-forward routes, no one was better. But when patience and cunning were required, no one was worse. Climbing, as it were, with blinders on, Tobin would sometimes claw his way into the most grievous jams. When he'd dead end, with nowhere to go and looking at a Homeric peeler, the full impact of his folly would hit him like a wrecking ball. He would panic, wail, weep openly and do the most ludicrous things. And sure enough, about 25 feet above the arch those sucker knobs ran out, and Tobin had nowhere to go.

To appreciate Tobin's quandary, recall what I've previ-ously mentioned about falls. He is 25 feet above the last piton, which means he's looking at a 50-foot fall, since a leader falls twice as far as he is above the last piece of protection. Remember, the belayer cannot take rope in during a fall because it happens too fast. He can only se-cure the rope—lock it off. But the gravest news was that I didn't think the piton I'd bashed under the roof would hold a 50-foot whopper. On really gigantic falls, the top piece often rips out, but the fall is broken sufficiently for a lower piece to stop you. In Tobin's case, the next lower piece was some dozen feet below the top one, at the rest hold, so in truth, Tobin was looking at close to an 80 footer, maybe more with rope stretch.

As Tobin wobbled far overhead, who should lumber up to our little group but his very father, a minister, a quiet, retiring, imperturbable gentleman who hacked and huffed from his long march up to the cliff side. After hearing so much about climbing from Tobin, he'd finally come to see his son in action. He couldn't have shown up at a worse time. It was like a page from a B-movie script—we, cringing and digging in, waiting for the bomb to drop; the good pastor, wheezing through his moustaches, sweat soaked and confused, squinting up at the fruit of his loins; and Tobin, knees knocking like castanets, sobbing pitifully and looking to plunge off at any second.

There is always something you can do, even in the grimmest situation, if only you keep your nerve. But Tobin was gone, totally gone, so mastered by terror that he seemed willing to die to be rid of it. He glanced down. His face was a study. Suddenly he screamed, "Watch me. I'm gonna jump."

We didn't immediately understand what he meant.

"Jump off?" Richard yelled.

"Yes!" Tobin wailed.

"NO!" we all screamed in unison.

"You can do it, Son," the pastor put in.

Pop was just trying to put a good face on it, God bless him, but his was the worst possible advice because there was no way Tobin could do it. Or anybody could do it. There were no holds. But inspired by his father's urging, Tobin reached out for those knobs so far to his right, now lunging, now hopelessly pawing the air.

And then he was off.

The top piton shot out and Tobin shot off into the grandest fall I've ever seen a climber take and walk away from—a spectacular, tumbling whistler. His arms flailed like a rag doll's, and his scream could have frozen brandy. Luckily, the lower piton held and he finally jolted onto the rope, hanging upside down and moaning softly. We slowly lowered him off and he lay motionless on the ground and nobody moved or spoke or even breathed. You could have heard a pine needle hit the deck. Tobin was peppered with abrasions and had a lump the size of a pot roast over one eye. He lay dead still for a moment longer, then wobbled to his feet and shuddered like an old cur crawling from a creek.

"I'll get it next time," he grumbled.

"There ain't gonna be no next time," said Richard.

"Give the boy a chance," the pastor threw in, thumping Tobin on the back.

When a father can watch his son pitch 80 feet down a vertical cliff, and straightaway argue that we were short-changing the boy by not letting him climb back up and have a second chance at an even longer whistler, we knew the man was mad, and that there was no reasoning with him. But the fall had taken the air out of the whole venture, and we were through for the day. The "next time" came four years later. In one of the most famous leads of that era, Ricky flashed the entire arch on his first try. Tobin and I followed.

Tobin would go on to solo the north face of the Matterhorn, the Walker Spur and the Shroud on the Grandes Jorasses (all in Levi's), would make the first Alpine ascent of the Harlin Direct on the Eiger, the first ascent of the Super Couloir on the Dru, would repeat the hardest free climbs and big walls in Yosemite and would sink his teeth into the Himalaya. He was arguably the world's most versatile climber during the late 1970s. But nothing really changed: He always climbed as if time were too short for him, pumping all the disquietude, anxiety and nervous waste of a normal year into each route.

I've seen a bit of the world since those early days at Tahquitz, have done my share of crazy things and have seen humanity with all the bark on, primal and raw. But I've never since experienced the electricity of watching Tobin out there on the quick of the long plank, clawing for the promised land. He finally found it in 1980, attempting a solo ascent of Mt. Alberta's North Face. His death was a tragedy. But I sometimes wonder if God Himself could no longer bear the strain of watching Tobin wobbling and lunging way out there on the sharp end of the rope, and finally just drew him in to the fold.

Many people discover climbing through hiking, backpacking or ski-mountaineering. Seeing the high crag and climbers on it, they tie into the rope to put some voltage into their wilderness experience. As climbing got more athletic, people tied in for other reasons. Some, like us, crossed over from traditional sports, with no deep calling from the great outdoors. That's where the crags were at, period. The cliff alone, and the climbing on it, was the draw. We'd drive, hitchhike, even walk to the trashiest areas—so long as there was rock. I climbed at 40-foot-high quarries hip-deep in defiled mattresses and rusting car bodies; bouldered next to mackerel canneries where clouds of carnivorous black flies cloaked every inch of stone; scaled bluffs rising from fetid lakes fed by sewage treatment plants, routes that could only be reached by canoes paddled through waters so odious and rife with "brown trout" it's a wonder we didn't perish just gaining the first belay. But as you travel and climb your way across the world, the landscape improves, and even the most focused climber will pause to admire the backdrop.

Perhaps it's a blinding strip of blue between two storm clouds, or a yucca in full bloom, that first grabs you; but once your eyes are opened, your heart follows the beat of a realm more encompassing than the steep side of a crag.

If you're young, climbing may give you your first taste of space and air and freedom, where all the music of a river or a hailstorm brings home the mysteries of nature. And as the vista broadens, so goes your wonder. I remember hanging 3,000 feet up on the great sodden wall of Angel Falls, where below and before us, rolling, mounting, sinking, rising, like huge swells in a huge green sea, the jungle fanned out to the edge of time. I remember hiking toward Carstenz Pyramid in New Guinea, where miles in the distance, outlined one against the other, the crests of a high cordillera seemed shuffled like a deck of stony cards—brusque peaks, bluish dips and notches, jutting arêtes swaying and rising and falling in the harsh light, more inaccessible as we mounted on. Maybe all at once, but more likely as your career unfolds, the actual climbing becomes just a refrain in an ever-changing fugue, where the trek through the measureless chasm and along the wild river becomes as prized and crucial as the most hard-fought summit.

I remember how our little band of Stonemasters would sack out—illegally, of course—in the forest below Tahquitz rock. Somebody would have filched a bottle from Pop's bar, and we'd build ourselves a drink, listening to the dead-soughing of the trees. It was always so quiet. Only the sound of wind, which carried with it the frank scent of bark and leaves and piquant red sap. Much more than the climbing, the forest could bring all things to calm within me and make my mind strong and sure, when those eerie emotions trembling between wonder and sorrow used to shiver through me from head to foot. Many times we fell asleep just as we lay, and did not wake till the birds came calling. Squinting up through the brace of trees we could see the distant white rock, and we would lie there for a while longer, wondering how we were ever made to be alive.

Our conversation never strayed far from Yosemite Valley, then the Mecca for every rock climber with a rope and a pair of boots. Hard-core climbers would scrimp and save and borrow and steal to make a summer pilgrimage to the place where legends were made and the big rocks were king. And king-sized. Monoliths like Mt. Watkins and El Capitan were over 3,000 feet high and the subject of fantastic tales of adventure. Just looking at the black-and-white photos in the old Yosemite guidebook, featuring tiny little men dangling up in the stratosphere on El Cap, would send jackals racing down my spine. I knew that not until I was up there slugging away, sleeping in a hammock and dealing with the "big air," would I find out once and for all if I had the stuff to be a real climber. Everything else, no matter the difficulty, was so much fluff.

Our climbing was progressing swimmingly, but Tahquitz, Suicide and Joshua Tree were, after all, practice areas compared to "the valley." We were counting the days until high school let out so we could have a shot at the big time. Working week nights at the gas station, and writing other people's term papers—really wretched ones—I salted away close to $300, and hoped that would see me through the whole summer in the valley. Meanwhile, as that last semester crept on like a glacier, we turned our attention to the unclimbed faces at Suicide.

Few climbers, even expert ones, have the confidence to start "putting up" new routes until they've been climbing for many years. An incident that happened some years later, in the cafeteria at Yosemite, illustrates my point.

I was with Canadian wall ace Hugh Burton. Only twenty-four, he'd already put up several new routes on El Capitan. A younger climber came to our table and asked Hugh for advice about bagging new big walls. Hugh suggested that our visitor go to some scrappy area where nobody ever climbed and experiment on short routes first. After he felt comfortable on one-pitch routes, perhaps then the young man could move on to bigger routes. Our guest, who already had a catalog of big walls to his credit, laughed. After all, he noted, the first new climb Hugh ever bagged was a grade-VI whopper on El Capitan. "True," Hugh stated, "but I didn't have to ask anyone how to do it."

To establish a new route is to make a timeless statement, a statement fixed in stone. While many climbers like the timeless part, knowing their name will live on in guidebooks, an equal number forget the statement bit. Making a bad statement, thus a bad route, is to smear your own name forever. So it's essential to do things right the first time around, particularly if bolts are placed. And the only way to climb those new faces at Suicide was to place bolts. The walls were smooth as a baby's butt, bereft of the tiniest sliver of a crack for a piton or a nut. Having now climbed hundreds of bolt-protected face routes, we understood the principals of a good face route, and in theory, how to fashion one. We knew what constituted a viable "line," all the subtle tricks of where and where not to place bolts ("engineering" the route), and had a good understanding of the accepted style of going about it. Of course, understanding how to do it, and actually doing it, are different things.

By definition, an adventure is any endeavour in which the ultimate outcome is completely unknown in advance. Accordingly, if you wanted to establish a new face climb, you started from the ground, met all difficulties as you climbed, and did it for the first time. Certainly, you could rope down from above and inspect the route, or try and climb it on a toprope strung from above. That way, you would know in advance if the climb was possible and could scope out the strategic knobs and edges where you potentially could stop and place the bolts, or you could even install them before trying the lead. But back then, such tactics were considered dirty pool and a wholesale act of cowardice, for the whole climbing game was based on the proviso that it was the first meeting between the climber and the given route—that you were climbing the route "on sight." The dignity of the on-sight ascent was the only thing that ensured an equal contest between the climber and the rock, thus preserving the all-important, traditional adventure element. The ground-up rule was not categorically followed, but when we broke it, we knew we were doing the devil's work.

A distinctive method evolved when we started bagging the new face routes. Somebody would pick the line, and an armada of friends would adjourn to the cliff. In later times, when nearly every inch of rock had been climbed (and new climbs required either a contrived effort, great imagination or a supreme technical performance), first ascents were undertaken with all the stealth of a bank heist, and you shared your project with a single partner. With the pickings so slim, and reputations to be made or broken, climbers would go to remarkable extremes to hoard the glory. But for our early efforts, we'd approach a new face climb five, even six strong. On really grim routes, you welcomed friends—the more the better—for hard work and danger are always more tolerable when shared. The unwritten law was to try to make the route as bold (dangerous) as you could.

These new face climbs were steep and inobvious, and in trying to figure just what line of holds to follow, falls, sometimes huge ones, were expected. You had to have protection, and in the absence of cracks for nuts or pitons, bolts were it. The rock is not a renewable resource, so any way you shake it, drilling holes into it and hammering home a bolt is a corruption comparable—in fact, worse—than dumping a heap of trash on the Appalachian trail. At least you can pick the trash up; the bolts are there till the Messiah returns. Accepting it as a necessary evil, the climber used to risk his hide to keep from placing too many, and all the jeering Pilates on the deck made sure of it. Here was a typical scenario:

Richard would have spotted, and in turn examined, what he thought was a potential new route. Half a dozen of us would trudge up to the rock and assemble at the base of the new project. Richard would tie in and cast off. No doubt the climbing is bleak from the first move, so after clawing up but a few body lengths, that little voice inside Richard's head is wisely suggesting he stop on his choice of obvious rest holds to sink the first bolt. That first one is critical, since it keeps the leader from "decking out," or hitting the ground. Of course, the shameless glee club piped up the second Richard's boot touched stone, now reflecting on his peerless technique, his Buddha-like calm on what, after all, was clearly easy climbing. At least he's made it look that way. So Richard ignores that little voice and presses on. Another 10 feet and that little voice is loud as the crack of doom, for he's looking at wrenched ankles at the least; and yet, if he is to believe the chorus below, he's in "tall cotton," is "looking superb" and in "total control." It is "no problem" for Richard. After another body length, his ears ringing with the sound of clashing pitchforks, Richard has reached his limit, and starts looking for a place to sink that first bolt.

The roar of "Not yet" nearly blows him off the holds. There is always "that knob," or that "big edge" he is so very close to—be it 5 or 50 feet above him—and the chorus, at no risk to themselves, is trying to shame him into forging on. After such a marvelous performance, it's no time for Richard to "chicken out." That first bolt has to be placed as high as possible "to keep the fluff off," to keep all but the most hard-core climbers off the route. You can't have just anybody repeating your masterpiece. Seeing that first bolt a country mile up, most parties will be scared away, the route will garner a serious reputation and all those associated with the first ascent would seem all the more heroic or daft, depending on your thinking.

Now Richard really does have his ass in a sling. There usually is a knob or an edge some ways above him, but the stretch between him and it might be the distance between shattered ankles and a pine box. But having already passed the other fifteen suitable rest holds, and in the absence of anything remotely adequate where he presently clings for his life, he now *has* to go for that higher knob if he ever hopes to stop and drill that bolt.

Remember that rocks are millions of years old, that rain and ice have coursed down them for eons. The sad result is that the top of a knob or edge that looks promising from below has often been severely rounded and worn by the elements. So here's Richard, scrapping up to what looks like a bomber hold only to find that a gekko couldn't stand on it without concern. Now it's trouble, big trouble. Real-izing his jam, the glee club is suddenly sympathetic with his plight. He gets only two hammer blows on the drill before he has to drop the gear and reset his screaming toes. By the time he finally sets the bolt and lowers off, it's taken him over an hour of trembling and cursing on that poor hold. His feet are numb, his fingers torn, his nerves shot and he's done for the day.

With the indemnity of the toprope, the next leader waltzes up to the high point in about ten seconds, and the chorus, with all the compassion of the hangman, fires back up. With the risk of hitting the ground eliminated, it's now time to really "run the rope." True, the wall is steep and smooth, and even an enormous fall should be a harmless "skidder," but the new leader is not keen to take one. Nevertheless the chorus hazes and browbeats him into climbing so far above the last bolt that he finally loses his very mind, stops to sink the bolt and is scourged as a wimp and a coward. After half an hour of wobbling and groaning and drilling, looking at a 50-foot fall if his left toe slips so much as a centimeter, he sinks the bolt, lowers off, is com-plimented on a "decent" job and another leader ties in for the same treatment. And on and on.

After someone finally reached the top, the team would often be so thrashed they'd have to return later to climb the route in one go. Sometimes it would take several days of fiendish work and many falls to drill and install all of the bolts before the route was ready for a proper lead. (It was rare but not unheard of that with all the work done, some cads would slip in and "steal" another team's new route, completing what others had started before they had a chance to return and polish it off themselves. Remarkable rivalries developed, sometimes resulting in lifelong grudges and even fistfights—which were serious affairs considering most climbers were young, extremely fit, and a little crazy to begin with. But all of this came later.)

Once the new route was completed, other climbers would repeat it. Perhaps it would become a classic. Future leaders would have to execute the same moves, but with the bolts already installed, the climb was a much tamer proposition. And if the first-ascent team "did themselves proud," future leaders, always goaded on by their own cadre of varlets on the ground, would claw up to each bolt and seize it like a lifesaver, marveling at the brave fool who had stood there and drilled it, looking at the mighty fall he nearly took just getting there.

Finally, and none too soon, high school let out. I didn't hang around for graduation, but was on the first Greyhound bus headed north for my first trip to Yosemite Valley.

Part Two

In an antique age, a glacier crept through a massive block of granite, leaving behind it a narrow valley whose floor is as flat as the surrounding walls are steep. As the world aged, a great pine forest burst forth to pronounce its green miracle: trees, colossal trees everywhere, from the high places to the edge of the Merced River, wending its way through the contours of a luxuriant grove. Along the river rest many bights and sandbars, peppered with mottled blond wood and polished boulders from the basement of time. From certain angles the image of the great walls burn on the slow-moving water. Most anywhere in the east end of the valley you can spot a silver strand shooting off the north wall and plunging into a magnificent bridled veil 3,000 feet below—Yosemite Falls, second largest in the world.

In midsummer, the view is choked by the smoke of countless campfires, hibachis, cars and tour buses; the river is a gridlock of sunburned drunkards in inner tubes and rafts, the ebbtide swirling with pop cans, dogs, guitars, flotsam of every class. But several miles distant from the hotels and campgrounds, El Cap meadow remains as pristine as it was a thousand years ago. Though the loop road runs through it—or along the edge of it—I've never seen one bit of trash there in over twenty years.

I once heard a naturalist claim the meadow was the work of a certain beetle that had ravaged the forest in recent times, leaving many square acres of shin-high grass in its wake. But there are old sepia photographs from the first visitors to the valley showing families of Miwok Indians in the meadow, grinding their meal in the shadow of the big rock. Anyone who stands out in the middle of this scenery of dreams knows he's at one of nature's most enchanted altars—like the brink of Niagara, or the southern rim of the Grand Canyon. To the south soars the orange bulk of Middle Cathedral. And to the north is El Capitan, blinding white and peerless in mass and magnificence. Though nearly half a mile away, it seems as though you can reach out and touch it. On any summer day, a raft of tourists are found gazing up at it—through opera glasses, binoculars, telescopes. The big, marvelous cliff captivates because it contains and reflects something of themselves. Their eyes naturally tilt up to the windblown summit and they imagine being up there, peering down into the void, and they shudder; for that void is beginning and end for everyone.

Suddenly, a tourist will yell, "There he is." All the others will crowd round and the man with the binoculars will point and describe the colors of clothes or a certain minaret, and the tourists will squint up, searching, and finally one will exclaim, "A man." Nowadays, it might well be a woman up there, a tiny mariner on a sea of rock, bulging haul bags moored close by, long loops of rope dangling below like threads. Above, the leader, seemingly frozen, is pasted to the side of a granite wave three miles long and 3,300 feet high. In early morning, when rags of fog drape the meadow and the air is still and sharp as knives, you can sometimes hear the tap, tap, tap of a hammer drumming up the dawn, a faint metronome of an ominous dance.

Ominous was the first impression I had when we barreled out of the tunnel at Inspiration Point, and El Capitan, five miles distant, first came into view. After an all-nighter on the Greyhound bus getting to Merced, I'd hitched a ride with a hayseed in an old Pontiac convertible. On leave from the army, Jimbo was a whippet-thin twenty-six-year-old, his teeth stained black by the bulging quid of snoose in his lower lip. Periodically spitting into a Folgers can between his legs, he drove like hell, hoping to find himself a "hussy" in Yosemite. He'd talked about girls and nothing but girls for 80 miles, yet when we rumbled out of that tunnel, Jimbo straightaway swerved into the pullout, sat up on the back of his seat and said, "Now *that's* a piece of rock." A few minutes later, Jimbo dumped me off at El Cap meadow.

I shouldered my two duffel bags, staggered out into the middle of the meadow and circled around, staring. It seemed impossible to take it all in, to appreciate the scale of things. I don't know if I was more amazed by the rocks or by the fact that I was finally among them. I lay down in the grass and fell asleep for a few hours, and when I woke up, the sun filled half the sky and my clothes were sweaty. At high noon in summer, the heat is so ferocious it drives even the gawkers away; but I spotted a man, over by the bank of the Merced, gazing up at the Cathedrals. He seemed part of the place, and I walked over to him, hoping to get directions to Camp 4.

The man was old and tired. He spoke in reedy gasps, his back so crooked with arthritis that he leaned against a tree for balance. Seeing the rope spilling from my duffel, his eyes sparkled and he pointed up and into the distance to a huge, tapering bullet of gray granite: Higher Cathedral Spire. I never understood if he had made the first ascent, some forty-five years before, or some later ascent; but a blind man could see what the climb meant to him. His body had decayed around him, but his heart hadn't aged a day since he stood proud on the summit, decades before. He didn't need to tell me he had come back for one last look. I got the directions, and left the old climber leaning against the tree, gazing up at the great gray spire.

*   *   *

In 1972, when I first stumbled into Yosemite, most climbers were dirt poor, a fact illustrated by the Camp 4 parking lot, an oily acre crammed with the proudest medley of heaps and rust buckets imaginable. Among the really prime rigs were an ancient British step-van that must have been parked on the street during the blitzkrieg; an old, dented, salt-pocked Cadillac, now a convertible thanks to a cutting torch; and a VW van, broad-sided, rear-ended and rolled, not a window in it, vice grips where the steering wheel should have been. Few of them ran without priming and a push start, if then. There wasn't a treaded tire in the whole lot, and a live battery got passed back and forth like a gold brick. The license plates were from Canada, Colorado, Wyoming, New York, most of these junkers having been babied down the road with little chance of reaching Yosemite, and no chance of ever leaving it. And for every heap in that lot, twenty just like it had been abandoned in flames on some lonesome highway, the plates stripped off and the driver, laden with ropes and bags, thumbing on toward Mecca.

Beyond the parking lot rested dozens of colorful tents, scattered like a fistful of jelly beans over a patch of dark forest. In the summertime, between two cinder block bathrooms at both ends of camp, many of the world's greatest climbers made their home there. Twenty years ago, "official" campsites were marked with a stake, or a number stenciled on a splintered picnic table, but there was never anybody to enforce these things. Other, legitimate campgrounds, full of scrubbed tourists and RVs and screaming brats, featured kiosks full of rangers who were full of silly rules, but during the first three summers I spent in Camp 4, I never saw a ranger. The park service considered it the biggest Babylon of rogues in California, and had essentially roped the place off. Only climbers stayed there. With no rangers and no rules, we were in hog heaven. In the almost complete absence of any women to sow some shame and keep discipline, the whole place was, in fact, an international ghetto.

There were German, British, French and Italian camps, where at night climbers could gather around the fire and lie to each other in their mother tongues. But partnerships were based more on temperament and ambition than nationality, so it was as standard to see a German climbing with an American, and a Mexican with a Pole, as it was to see a purely national rope—or campsite. While the German and French sites were clean and ordered, the American and British camps were always disasters—strewn with pots and pans and beer bottles, "fur" books, dumbbells, blaring radios and unidentified trash.

With the regularity of Old Faithful, mornings and afternoons, a double-decker tour bus would chug down the road bordering Camp 4. The tour guide was always a confidante of the climbers, and was always bored as an angel, reciting the same spiel to the same crowd; so it was natural and inevitable that a certain diversion evolved. Working the microphone, babbling about John Muir and Teddy Roosevelt, the guide would start in about the "bold Yosemite climbers," which was our cue. Pointing to the flaking ghetto, seventy-five wide-eyed tourists would often see one of the bold climbers, pants around his ankles, mooning the double-decker. And the guide would go on, never missing a beat.

I'd been beaten to Camp 4 by The Stonemasters' reputation, dragged there by a partner of Bud Couch's named Jim Doninni, an accomplished, thirty-year-old Yosemite climber who for several seasons had tuned up at Tahquitz and Suicide before heading to the valley for the summer. Down in Idyllwild, Jim had bouldered with our little group enough to know we were all insolent loudmouths, and I hadn't gotten ten steps into Camp 4 when I ran into him, heading off to climb.

"So you made it," he said drolly, dropping his pack and giving me the once over. He did everything but lick his chops. If we had been a little more low key down in Idyllwild, I remember thinking, Jim would have let me walk right on past. Then I could have enlisted some other new-comer and slipped into the program nice and easy–like. Jim thrust his chin toward a shirtless, muscular specimen sitting on a boulder and said to him, "The kid's name is Long. John Long. He needs a partner." Jim chuckled, shouldered his pack, and disappeared.

My new acquaintance had a vulpine smile and a gymnast's frame and there seemed something familiar about his profile. But he seemed so unassuming I thought nothing more about it.

"Put your stuff over there," he said, pointing to a nearby campsite. "We got room."

I dragged my duffels over, sat down at the picnic table and started talking with my new friend who appeared to be somewhere in his late twenties. He asked me about my climbing down south, which I related with enthusiasm, stretching a few points to hop up the conversation. Somewhere in there I detected a certain interview quality to our dialogue, and after a few minutes, I was certain I'd seen his face somewhere before.

"So, what should we climb?" he asked.

"We?"

"You wanna go climbing, don't you?"

Hell yes, I did, and without thinking about it, I suggested the Left Side of Reed's Pinnacle. I'd never seen Reed's Pinnacle, and didn't know the left side from the right side. I only knew Bud Couch had failed on the left side, and figured if I got that route behind me, I'd have a leg up on Bud and Yosemite.

"Get your stuff," my new friend said, crawling into a tent and tossing out several rucksacks full of gear. When I saw the name "Bridwell" on one of the packs, I froze like a deer caught in headlights.

Jim Bridwell—"The Bird," as we later styled him—was the biggest name in American climbing, perhaps world rock climbing. He had burst onto the Yosemite scene in much the same way we'd stormed Idyllwild, coming on the heels of a retiring generation of Yosemite greats. That generation was the first to climb the mighty big walls, inventing the techniques as they went along. These routes thrust American rock climbers ahead of the Europeans, and as these giants slipped off the cutting edge, around 1969, only The Bird kept the art from slipping back into a period of genre painting.

In a manner, a rope ran from Jim back to the very beginnings of the sport—for he'd climbed with Kor, who had climbed with Robbins, who had climbed with Wilts, who had climbed with Mendenhall, who had climbed with Clyde, and for all I knew, the only thing separating me from Edwin Whymper and the first ascent of the Matterhorn was the half hour before I could rope up with The Bird.

We hitchhiked to Reed's Pinnacle, a 300-foot exfoliating slab leaning against a vertical wall of smooth gray granite. The slab's left side described a soaring crack, beginning with a wide chimney, which I led. The hard climbing in

▲▲▲

Pioneers

Between 1420 and 1620 European mariners learned that all seas are one sea, that seamen, given adequate ships and stores, skill and courage, could in time reach any country in the world that had a coast, and—what was more important—return home. Historians loosely refer to this epoch as "The Age of Discovery," when immortals like Columbus, John Cabot, Vasco da Gama, Drake, Balboa and Coronado spearheaded the discovery of new worlds. While refinements in navigation and seamanship were rapid and comprehensive during this era, men had been sailing the high seas for over two thousand years; so the immortal mariners were not, in fact, inventing navigation, and their accomplishments were much more feats of vision, courage and, to some extent, luck, than they were merely technical triumphs. On many early voyages of discovery, many captains considered it even money that the ship and all hands on it was going to sail off the very edge of the world, would be vacuumed up by terrible waterspouts, would get swallowed whole by monsters of the deep. The outcome of these adventures was totally unknown for they were first into new and unknown seas.

To an extent, the Yosemite pioneers shared many similarities with the ancient mariners. Rock climbing, in a generic sense, was already well established by the time Royal Robbins, Jerry Gallwas and Mike Sherrick first scaled the Northwest Face of Half Dome in 1957 (the first Yosemite wall). New techniques were invented, and wall climbing entered its golden age, when all the largest formations were first climbed (from 1957 to 1965). Granted, techniques were refined in the process, but the first ascent of the big walls was much more a victory of spirit than one of technical prowess. The terrain was completely unchartered, the outcome was anything but known. On several occasions, first-ascent parties found themselves so committed that they could not retreat, that the only way off was up. Over a period of less than ten years, routes were pushed up the great faces of El Capitan, Half Dome, Sentinel,

Leaning Tower, Washington Column, Mt. Watkins, Quarter Dome, Ribbon Falls and Upper Yosemite Falls. Names like Warren Harding, Royal Robbins, Chuck Pratt, Tom Frost, Yvon Chouinard, Steve Roper, Layton Kor, TM Herbert and a handful of others will always be revered among climbers, so long as climbers understand what these pioneers actually did.

▲

Idyllwild tended toward steep face routes, so my crack technique was needy, and I tried to bluster by with brute strength. This worked fine for that first pitch, a moderate squeeze job ending atop a small, tight stance beneath a horrific-looking "off-size" crack. It's a terrible thing to cringe below a ghastly crack that soars overhead like your worst enemy, and not know what the devil you're doing. The situation was altogether different for The Bird, who arrived at my stance, flashed that smile again and led off without a word.

Yosemite is the crack-climbing capitol of the world. For reasons Bridwell couldn't explain, soaring, razor-cut fissures bisect virtually every face, big and small, sometimes bottom to top. There are techniques for climbing all cracks but none so dreadful and tricky as that necessary for the hateful "off-size."

The Bird chugged fluidly up the second, crux pitch, and was easily 60 feet off the belay before he placed the first piece of protection—a dinky, wired nut behind a wafer-thin flake. Above, the crack pinched down to about five inches wide, and he slithered effortlessly on. About 30 feet below the next belay, the wired nut fell out, and not a single piece of protection lay between us, a distance of over 80 feet. I hesitated to yell up the dire news, but did. The Bird paused, chuckled, and said, "Relax, kid. I might as well be walking on a sidewalk." When The Bird went to work, the climb didn't have a chance. He waltzed up the last bit of the gruesome crack, set the anchor, and the rope came snug round my waist. My turn.

The trick to these cracks is to keep a prudent pace, resting and spurting in turn, so you climb a series of short pitches instead of one long and grisly one. But on this climb there was no place to rest—at all. The crack was too big for fists, too small for a shoulder. My knee didn't fit, though I nearly ground my patella off trying to force it inside. My feet were bicycling around and when I'd try to jackknife up a move, I'd slip down two, fiendishly arm-barring, but buttering slowly out. I was sort of swimming inside the crack—or rather, thrashing like a drowning man—yanking out on the lip so hard I thought I'd pull the whole damn pinnacle off the wall.

This kind of climb has a cumulative effect that asserts itself suddenly, and I'd battled to within five feet of The Bird when all at once my body felt as if it'd just swallowed about three yards of quick-set cement. According to the old adage, you never learn anything until you're "pumped." I'd either learn in a hurry, or fall off and lose face forever.

"Out right," The Bird instructed.

My hand shot out to a knob on the otherwise blank face; I braced, got my knee locked higher, ratcheted up, stretched and at arm's length, grabbed the ledge and floundered onto it, spent.

"Done many off-widths?" The Bird drolled.

"Hundreds," I wheezed. He handed me the rack, and I led up the last pitch, a perfect hand crack.

So began a friendship that would take Jim and me up many big walls together, from the jungles of South America

▲▲▲

Climbing Cracks

"Jamming" is the basic method for climbing cracks. On finger cracks (⅜ inch to ½ inch wide), the climber slots his fingers into almost imperceptible variances in the crack, often jockeying the digits, trying for a good, snug fit above a slight constriction. When pulled down upon, the meat or knuckles of the fingers lock in the constriction, the feet making do with whatever is available on the face. Extreme finger cracks are often so thin and shallow that only the fingertips—sometimes just the pinkies—find purchase in the crack. It's rough duty on the cuticles.

An "off-finger" crack (¾ inch wide) is where the crack is just a hair too wide to twist your fingers into, yet still too small to accept your whole hand. The fingers rattle hopelessly inside the crack, yet the knuckles keep the palm of the hand outside. Here, the fingers are draped over each other, "stacked," bunched and/or torqued on by placing the hand, index finger down, in the crack and cranking the wrist and arm down. The thumb is sometimes lodged between the tip and the first knuckle—anything to make the fingers somehow fit. Once the crack opens up enough for a "hand jam" (usually 1½ inches to 2 inches wide), most any angled rock is climbable, even the underside of roofs. By cupping the hand and expanding it—the heel of the hand and the fingers on one side of the crack, the back of the hand on the other—a surprisingly secure "jam" is accomplished. With practice, a good hand jam is as secure as hanging on a pull-up bar. In turn, the feet are twisted into the crack as well, and even dead-vertical hand cracks are, for the true expert, ascended with the ease of walking up a stepladder. A little bigger crack, and it's "fist-jamming." The harder you squeeze the fist inside the crack, the more it expands. Fist jamming can torch the forearms, but the technique is quite secure once mastered.

"Off-width," aka "off-size," technique begins once the crack is too wide to fist-jam (usually beyond 4 inches wide), as was the case on the Left Side *of Reed's Pinnacle. Since the crack is too large to cam or lodge any part of your upper body, you must employ a variety of "arm-bar" configurations, levering with the arm inside the crack, the back of the elbow on one side, the palm on the other, while trying to lock the knee—if width allows—and twist the feet so the heel and toe are lodged on opposing sides. Moving up is accomplished by locking the upper body off, pulling the legs up and resetting them, then ratcheting the upper body up, ad nauseam. The technique is technical and strenuous. Most pictures of climbers struggling up grim off-width cracks show someone seemingly trying to force his body through a crevice that is too small for him. Solid off-width technique requires many climbs to perfect, for the various body positions and confusing counterpressures required are about as natural as walking on your hands. The first few efforts are invariably villainous, thrashing epics resulting in bad abrasions and tweaked muscles.*

to Borneo and beyond; and it all started on that oily crack at Reed's Pinnacle.

Within a week (school was now out across the country), Camp 4 was packed. Of the hundreds of climbers, about six or seven others—of roughly my age and ability—had gone through a trial by fire with The Bird, and we sort of fell in together. Aside from my Idyllwild partners, Ricky and Richard, there was Mark Chapman, with his poet's soul, simian strength and a voice like Frank Sinatra; and Eric Shoen (aka "Mellow Brutus"), who was strong enough to rip your head off at the waist, but never would since he got weepy over stray dogs and kids on crutches. He went at about six foot two, 220 pounds, and had the odd distinction of being the finest Jewish free climber in the world. And, of course, Rik Reider, a flame-redhead with a cowlick his barber didn't understand. He had the talent to change climbing forever, but the following year on El Capitan, falling rocks fractured his skull and put him out of climbing forever. God only knows what Rik would have accomplished had he lasted a couple more summers. And then there was Dale Bard—one part anorectic brat, two parts dynamite, three parts climbing fanatic. Despite a strict diet of wild honey, hot chocolate and Snickers bars, Dale was so lean and whey-faced you wanted to ask about his embalmer. Over the next ten years, Dale would climb El Capitan more than forty times. (Dale once told me "There's more to life than climbing, you know." "Yeah, like what?" I asked. "I don't know," he said, "so it can't be much.") Later came Kevin Worrel, Ed Berry, Billy Westbay and others. We were all The Bird's boys.

The Bird was a skilled teacher and a passable storyteller, so we got the rudiments and the tales at one go. Mostly, he demystified the process by taking us, or directing us, onto the legendary routes we'd so long dreamed about. His knack was to keep us entertained while enriching our curriculum. But never mind the father business. The Bird had big plans, and to see them through he had to pull a couple of us up to his level—no easy trick, since Jim Bridwell was probably the finest all-around rock climber on the planet. His method was unadorned: He'd snag the most promising kids in camp, climb them till they couldn't climb anymore, then tie them back in and climb them some more. He wanted to find out what our maximum was, how much we could take. And he got it all. He never eased us into anything, and never worried about teaching us more than we could learn. Too little time for that. We'd either get world-class in a hurry, or fall away like chaff. In this manner he was able to shift the sands of daydreams until he produced the solid stuff—the best climbers and the greatest ascents of the era.

Most of The Bird's boys slept on the ground. The Bird, however, had a tent—a sprawling, green-canvas affair—the kind Ike used to tenant in the European theater. When The Bird was handling some personal business inside, he'd hang a cardboard sign on the zippered door: KEEP OUT. This went for tourists, fellow climbers, park rangers, the president of the United States and Jehovah. By morning, the sign usually was gone, and in the faint musk of perfume and Tawny Port, a little group of us would hunker down inside and discuss various routes, getting The Bird's feedback as to climbs particularly germane to our curriculum. Of course we broached other topics besides climbing, though The Bird did most of the talking because he was just enough older than we that he seemed to know everything (he claimed to have known The Unknown Soldier, and who shot him). He looked on Yosemite like it was created for him alone—plus a few of his friends.

Anyway, after an hour or so, we'd splinter off into groups of two or three and fan out across the valley to the Crack of Despair, Twilight Zone, Chopper Flake, New Dimensions, Outer Limits, Lunatic Fringe.

Though a route may receive a purely arbitrary name, it generally suggests something of the physical characteristics of the climb, and the psychological perils of leading it. (Names like "Dwindling Greenbacks," and "She Loves Me Not" tell other stories.) A party will often choose—or refuse—a climb simply by its name, and the climbers who established it.

" 'The Meat Grinder'?" somebody would question. "Oh, it's a Robbins route," a partner would say, and we instantly had a whole rucksack full of connotations. Robbins was a bold climber. Everybody knew that. And The Meat Grinder sounded beastly. Better leave it for next season. Then The Bird would chime in: "Robbins climbed that route in the rain, in hiking boots, fifteen years ago. John, Eric—you're on it. Bring a couple big nuts for the third pitch."

So Eric and I would hitchhike to some vague bend in the road to start the half-hour trek to The Meat Grinder. We'd get lost ten times thrashing through labyrinthine forests and sandy riverbeds, end up in the wrong canyon, do more thrashing to finally find the route, spend five hours clawing up a climb that was supposed to take three, take several wrenching falls off the crux, get off route and fall again to finally wheeze and rattle to the top and collapse in a skinned heap, wondering how the devil Royal Robbins ever climbed that wicked route in the rain and in hiking boots. (Both were outright lies.) Then, it was straight back to The Bird's tent. We'd lay around on lush cushions and, after the last of The Bird's boys had stumbled back home, the lying would begin.

A climber could wobble into that tent as beleaguered as Job, and virtually pass out; yet his barked knees, raw elbows and split, oozing fingertips were never the direct result of a climb perhaps a little too hard for him. Rather, there was "moss in the crack," or the face was wet, or too dry, too slick, too grainy. But never too hard. The actual climb always "went fine," and was, in fact, easier than expected. Blowing smoke rings at the canvas ceiling, The Bird would inquire about a certain roof or flare that might have contributed to a shotgun-type wound on somebody's forearm, but the stricken climber would wave it off with a flick of the bleeding hand, then go back to sleep.

In looking back, I realize that The Bird pushed us to the brink, but no further. The toils of a young climber battling his way up his first world-class climbs are so huge that he deserved never to be chided for his honest failures, when he'd try and try and simply could not do something. The Bird was quick to mention there was always another day. More than once, he'd join in the next attempt to orchestrate, if not lead, the climb himself.

In some ways we were like mercenaries crawling back from some small, desperate and distant war, able to talk to and understand only other veterans. Who else knew or cared about a secret war in an obscure land, about the painful sacrifices with their moments of private bravery by unknown heroes? Who else had even *heard* about the battle? But we never felt like heroes. Lying flat on our backs and licking our wounds, we often wondered just who had won.

Though Bridwell and I would go on to do many adventures together, it's difficult to separate the romantic conception I had of him at eighteen and the man he really was. It takes a rare kind of generosity for someone to nurture a community unto itself, a sort of closed circle of friends similarly engaged; and that is what Bridwell did, and generous is the only way to describe him. He'd give his friends the shirt off his back, and did. He never made the slightest show of his reputation, never tried to act like he was any better than the rest of us. Whenever visiting climbers came up to shake his hand or perhaps to exchange a few words with the legend, he'd more often than not tell them to grab their stuff because *they* were going climbing. In quiet moments, he was reflective and sometimes melancholy and envious of the world we were not a part of. But there was never a doubt in his mind that he was following his chosen path, and that it was his unalterable fate to do so. Talent is not a rare thing. But a champion is, and like Robbins before him, Bridwell was all of a champion. It takes a lot of failures to become a champion, just like it takes a lot of living to know why this is so. And so in the end, Jim Bridwell was humble enough to take in a group of wayward kids and point them in the right direction. There were other big-name climbers around, certainly; but they couldn't be bothered to fiddle around with us punks. And when we passed them all by, one by one, it was the humility we had inherited from The Bird that let us move past gracefully.

Day-to-day living in Camp 4 was coarse business. Most of it I can explain away to the shamelessness of youth; but some bits were poor form by any measure, and excuses won't do so I won't even try.

Our standard abode was a four-man expedition tent, often "borrowed," or bought secondhand from another climber who had either borrowed it himself, or gotten it as a perk for some expedition. No one I knew had actually gone to a retail store and bought one. Even twenty years ago, high-tech tents cost hundreds of dollars—which none of us had—and you simply had to have one to safeguard your few possessions against sudden and violent thunderstorms. Understand that *four man* refers to an area sufficient to allow four beanpoles to sleep on their sides, with not space enough between them to drive a knifeblade. So in fact a four-man tent was just big enough for *one* climber to inhabit with some elbow room.

It didn't matter to us what we slept on, as far as padding went; but if we had any hopes of luring a girl into our tent to "thread a little pipe," then we had to have a mattress. These were acquired almost exclusively from girls who worked as maids in the various park hotels, lodges and tent cabins. Since we could not pinch the precious mattresses outright, we had to barter for them, and such transactions took many and curious forms.

My buddy Ron K. rebuilt a girl's carburetor in exchange for a mattress; Tim P. guided a lady up the East Buttress of Middle Cathedral, got pinned on the summit in a thundershower and had to bivouac with no gear, starving and freezing in the rain, the girl cursing him through the livelong night—all for his feather bed (from which he got crabs); and there was a maid, one Tina Y., a vinegary debutante who was about five feet tall in boots and weighed well over two bills, had a tongue like a paring knife and who "bucked like a mule and snored like a chainsaw," according to Howie R. Howie was not the only climber who swapped a long night with Tina for a secondhand mattress.

Most of The Bird's disciples were about eighteen, when other boys our age were tooling around in hot rods and trying to inveigle the neighbor girl out of her Levi's. There were no hot rods in the Camp 4 parking lot, but since it was summertime, the valley was always full of girls; and our craving to get laid cannot be overstated. However, the Yosemite climber worked the field at a disadvantage—90 cents away from having a buck, ragged as a roach, eating the holes out of doughnuts and trying to woo Helen of Troy. That he might end up with someone a little less was to be expected; that he ended up with anyone at all was a miracle. But young people have a way of ending up together no matter the circumstances. Sometimes we got lucky. I often wonder how the girls felt about a bunch of rascals who understood it was their pleasure that counted.

It's hysterical to recall how some climbers tooled out their tents in the hopes of creating a romantic atmosphere. Some had "stereo" sound systems, consisting of various two-bit radios, tuned to the same station and positioned about the tent; others had pictures of schmaltzy sunsets or portraits of Pan and Venus de Milo or even pink cupids taped and even stapled to the nylon walls; still others hung bead curtains and small mirrors, burned incense or had fancy bedding (Bernie fleeced the purple satin sheets and pillows from a whorehouse in Blue Diamond, Nevada—swank merchandise, save for the stains). Of course the crux was always getting the girl *into* the tent in the first place, and more than one would-be darling found the decor so ludicrous that the amour never got past the rain fly. (Female climbers were starting to ease into the scene, thanks to climbers like Beverly Johnson, Anne Rizzi, Julie Bruger and Katherine Cullane, whose exploits on both grim free climbs and big walls were destroying the silly notion that the rocks were only for the boys. Later came Lynn Hill and Mari Gingery, who could easily climb with the best of us. Someday I hope to see a book like this one from the female perspective.)

The business of eating was, remarkably, even more important than getting laid. Most all climbers were appallingly hungry young men. Food was fuel, and we burned immense amounts of it, judging all meals by quantity, not quality. Ninety percent of a climber's money went to buying food, the other 10 percent for liquor. Every "campsite" had a thrashed old picnic table usually shared by four climbers. Each table had a smattering of pots and pans—black as stovepipes—plus a Coleman stove that broke down so often and so entirely that every Camp 4 climber knew those stoves as well as their own hands.

Meals were one-course affairs. The favorite was a sort of goulash consisting of rice and spuds as the principal ingredient, enriched with anything else you had to chuck into the mix—canned vegetables, meat, acorns, even pie filling—anything to sweeten the pot. The trick was to keep the stove going and to keep stirring the bubbling gunk so that it

didn't burn. Once the fare was judged "done," we all tore
into it. The secret was to eat until you felt ready to explode,
rest for a bit and then eat some more. It was standard to see
several climbers lying on the ground following a particularly wholesome graze, so bloated we couldn't hope to even
stand.

A favorite stunt was to frequent barbecues and picnics
put on by various religious groups who swarmed into the
park for weekend retreats. These gatherings were mostly
private affairs, though strangers were sometimes tolerated
so long as the spirit of the thing was close to their heart
(if you could suffer through a sermon and the singing of
hymns and so forth). Acting pious and playing along was
our ticket to the chow—which was plentiful, if nothing
else. It's mortifying to reflect back on us, all turned out
in our finest Levi's and T-shirts, smiling through a tor-
turous homily and crooning along with the righteous, the
whole time licking our chops and growing increasingly
restive until we could finally break for the vittles like a
pack of wolves. These celebrations were generally large,
well-organized and well-stocked, and our numbers were
comparatively so small that we could eat like we were going to the gas chamber and no one cared. But I remember
one time things got really ugly.

Like I said, we usually tried to keep our numbers down
to half a dozen or so—just The Bird's hard-core little
band—but this time the word had gotten out, and about
twenty of Camp 4's hungriest showed up for a stiff affair
put on by the Four Square Pentecostal Church. We be-
longed there like an arrowhead belongs on the moon, and
everyone knew it—especially the pastor, a vast, blustery
Southerner who strung us out for hours. Once the feed
finally got underway, the climbers stampeded straight over

the faithful and began shoveling down beans and potato salad straight from great vats, scarfing fried chicken with both hands and right off the trays, swilling punch directly from the jugs, crashing the line over and over before the proper crowd had eaten so much as a carrot stick.

I don't remember what set the whole thing off, only that one of us cut the line for the tenth time, reaching for a last drumstick or something, and someone angrily grabbed his arm. Words were exchanged; there was some pushing and, as the shocking news spread that the food was all gone, we scattered into the surrounding forest. I had so many franks and ribs and rhubarb pies on board I could barely walk. I caught up with The Bird in the darkness of the forest, and we both leaned against a tree and glanced back. The dust had cleared and the big pastor was up on a picnic table, sweat pouring off his bald pate like the rivers of Damascus. He glared down at the great mountain of bones and rinds and corn cobs strewn about him. Then looking at the starving faithful, he threw up his hands and cried, "Christ almighty, folks. The famine is sore in the land!"

"Stolen waters are sweet," said The Bird, stumbling away.

Because Yosemite Valley was the axis on which rock climbing then spun, the particular style laid down in the early seventies has persisted to the present day, and I imagine young climbers are still crashing other people's picnics. During a recent visit to Camp 4, climber/writer Jon Krakauer thought he had entered a time warp: the red bandannas, the baggy white pants, the long hair, the Allman Brothers blasting from radios. All these things are still there in force, much the same as they were twenty years ago. For the most part, I'm grateful I was there when the die was cast.

While much of the old milieu still lives on, some of our

original group did not survive our first few months in the valley. In body, yes; but more than a few either stopped coming to Bridwell's big tent, or slipped out of the valley like bandits, never returning. Sore fingers, a bad fall, a broken heart, feelings that life was passing them by drove many would-be champions off. Plus, the physical demands were so enormous that almost any alternative, even digging ditches, seemed attractive. But other factors were at work as well.

Most of the dropouts came into the world better off than the rest of us. They could afford to go about things casually, because they were already somebody, or were the sons of somebody. They didn't *need* climbing. Their fathers assured them that good citizens didn't abandon society for three months at a pop, mingle with riffraff in an outdoor ghetto and plan their days to the beck and call of a muscular bohemian named Jim Bridwell. The rest of us were nobodies from nowhere with nothing but each other, nobodies who saw climbing as a means to change that. We welcomed the chance to postpone our adult lives to try to make history on the big rocks, history that meant something only to us. A few climbers were locked into the program body and soul, but had to drop out just the same, none more reluctantly than Nate Pettibone.

Nate blew into Yosemite one weekend and immediately made a big splash. Turned out like the lead singer for the Funkadelics, he wore tie-dyed pants (that appeared expertly tailored, though not necessarily for him), rose-colored shades and an enormous earring he claimed was diamond, though it cracked when The Bird raked it across a wine bottle. Straight out of the Dust Bowl, he spoke with such an Okie-burr we could scarcely understand him. He was, bar none, the strongest climber I'd ever seen. For that first month, Nate settled in splendidly, leading some of the hardest climbs in the valley. Then things started to go. First, a finger tendon. Next his elbows. Finally, both shoulders. His muscles were simply stronger than what his tendons could take. As Ricky said, "He wanted to be Jimi Hendrix, but the strings broke." Nate thumbed back to Oklahoma, and it was later said he was doing thirty years at Folsom for counterfeiting, was a stock car racer, had a heart transplant, was a cook on a submarine. In fact, we never heard from Nate again.

Nate was the exception, though it's amazing now to look back and realize the hardships we endured as a matter of course. I plowed through the toughest times more out of ignorance to the fact that I was suffering than by virtue of some special steel. I remember one time when Ron Fawcett and I spent an entire morning thrashing around the steep slopes above the Cookie Cliff, looking for a certain infamous crack. It was 90 degrees in the shade. We didn't bring enough water. We never found the crack. Hiking back to the road, I was thirsty enough to drink seawater. We stumbled across a small creek. The water looked a little dark, smelled strange, tasted worse, so I drank just enough to slacken my throat. Ron didn't drink. That night I was just settling into my bag when my works started churning. Then the light sweat all over and the queasiness and malarial trembling that assures you you're shortly going to be throwing up for real. I needed some place to go and see this work through, but no such place was handy. So I grabbed a gallon jug of water, and in only a pair of nylon gym trunks, trekked off behind camp to a moraine field about a quarter mile away. It was pitch black and I continuously fell and wrenched and barked this or that, and barely made the moraine when I started retching. Hard. Then came the diarrhea. I stripped naked and the business quickly curled me into a fetal knot, gushing from both ends. Then it started raining. Just a light drizzle at first. Then like Sumatra during the monsoon. I kept wallowing there, gasping down slugs from the water bottle and retching in turn, and it went on for hours. Finally, I got that euphoric feeling when you know the body has at last flushed itself pure. I lay in the pounding rain for a while longer to regain my wits and a little strength. Then I stood up and raised my arms and the squall washed me as clean as the day I was born. I slipped back into my trunks and made my way back to camp, figuring I'd managed the affair pretty shrewdly. I woke up feeling not so bad at all. A bowl of Cheerios, and Ron and I were back looking for that crack, found it, and bagged the third ascent. Now I understand why kids make the best soldiers. Nobody else can hack it.

With each passing week, our little group grew tighter, every one of us locked into a kind of freemasonry. After two months, The Bird's troops were down to about six. No longer did we stagger back into the big tent more dead than alive. We were getting "dialed in." But no matter how well we fared on the difficult free climbs, the onus of the big walls, and the fact we had yet to challenge them, hung round our necks like millstones. You can scrape and claw your way up the most horrendous little routes in the world, and feel pretty good about yourself; but you can only drive past El Capitan, can only stand out in the meadow and gaze up at it so many times, before you know the genuine fleece is nowhere else.

By August that first summer, Richard, Ricky and I had bagged a couple of short walls—quick, steep affairs on Washington Column. We had the procedures down: how to haul the bags; how to erect a string of creaky pitons; how

▲▲▲

Grades

The decimal rating system (5.0 to 5.14 for free climbing, A1 to A5 for artificial or "aid" climbing) tells free climbers how difficult a climb is. The attending grade rating tells how much time an experienced climber will take to complete a given route:

     Grade I   *One to three hours.*

     Grade II   *Three to four hours.*

     Grade III   *Four to six hours. A strong half day.*

     Grade IV   *Full day. Emphasis on full.*

     Grade V   *One to two days. Bivouac is usually unavoidable.*

     Grade VI   *Two or more days on the wall.*

The decimal rating is a relatively objective appraisal of difficulties, usually arrived at through consensus. The grade rating is posited as objective, but it uses the theoretical "experienced climber" as the example of how long a given route should take. Compare the grade rating with the par rating on a golf course. A par 5 means a honed golfer can probably hole the ball in five shots, rarely less, but a hacker will smile at a bogey six. Likewise, a world-class team in top form can usually crank a grade V in one day, whereas the intermediate climber had best come prepared to spend the night.

While the rather generic term big wall *is used to indicate any massive sweep of steep rock, climbers have traditionally considered only a grade-VI route to be a genuine big wall. Grade V's are considered "small walls," regardless of how big they actually are, because* big *here refers more to how long it takes than the actual height of the formation.*

▲

Jeff Perrin (top) and Peter Takeda
on El Capitan's Sunkist route in Yosemite. (Greg Epperson)

John Bachar in 1987.
(Chris Falkenstein)

From left, Jim Bridwell, Billy Westbay and John Long stand below
El Capitan in 1975 after pioneering the first single-day ascent
of the wall. (The Billy Westbay Collection)

John Long on the
Lost Arrow Spire.
(Bob Gaines)

Bob Gaines, John Long and Dwight Brooks on the Lost Arrow Spire. (The Bob Gaines Collection)

John Flynn and Mike Corbett
on Lost Arrow.
(Chris Falkenstein)

Mike Corbett on El Cap's Nose.   (Chris Falkenstein)

Mark Wellman (right) and Mike Corbett
on day eleven of their climb of Half Dome in Yosemite
(Chris Falkenstein)

John Mather making his way across
Lost Arrow's Tyrolean Traverse.
(Chris Falkenstein)

The author atop Yosemite's Glacier Point.

(Bob Gaines)

to spend the long night "sleeping" in hammocks strung to the vertical wall, 1,000 feet of air below us. The moment had come to try it all on the grandest scale. I chose The Nose route on El Capitan, one of the first true big walls climbed in Yosemite, and still the most famous.

November 12, 1958. Warren Harding, George Whitmore and Wayne Merry are lashed to a hanging stance 3,150 feet up El Capitan. The days are cold and short, and already afternoon shadows streak up the wall beneath them. They gaze overhead and wonder: Will we *ever* get off? Will it *ever* be over?

On this, their final push, the trio has been on the wall eleven days, twice as long as any American has ever spent on a rock climb. Below in the shadows lies a tale of forty-five days spread over eighteen months, each day a pitched battle, every lead sieged. They've met obstacles no rock climber has ever seen, let alone mastered—wild pendulums, expanding flakes thin as flapjacks, plus the back-breaking task of hauling vast supplies up the cliff side. And now, only a 50-foot headwall bars them from the top of the mightiest rock wall in the contiguous United States. But that headwall, that last 50 feet, is dead blank and severely overhanging. They'll have to retreat 350 feet to Camp 6 and a good ledge, and tackle the headwall in the morning.

There comes a time in all great climbers' careers when technique or fitness or even genius falls short, when only brute willpower can close the deal. Harding considers his swollen hands, the mangled gear and frayed ropes, the rats that gnawed through haul bags, the rain and sleet and chilling retreats, his running feuds with rangers, the private terrors and sleepless nights and yet just now, hanging in a web of tattered slings, he can nearly spit to the top.

Warren Harding is not going down.

As darkness sets in, Harding starts bolting. And in an epic no climber should ever forget, he hammers through the night, finally punches home the twenty-eighth and last bolt, and stumbles to the top just as dawn spills into Yosemite Valley. The first ascent of The Nose, one of the greatest, and certainly the most-sought-after pure rock climb in the world, is a done thing.

For my first trip up El Cap, I teamed up with British ace Ron Fawcett, who was probably the finest free climber in Europe, and would be for a decade to come. My age (nineteen), he too was principally a crag climber looking to extend his repertoire. We'd been climbing together for some weeks, doing short, hard free climbs, and feeling proud about life; but each time we passed El Cap, we'd glance at each other like thieves because the amplitude of that rock, and the towering challenge it presented, totally overshadowed the silly little routes we were bagging.

So long as we pursued the dream, we felt we were dangling on the lip of heroism; but we were doing neither on the short routes. The dream was *not* 150 feet high. It was a mile high and profoundly dramatic. The short routes were exciting, but excitement was a poor substitute for the theater of doom found on the big walls, and we both knew it.

One day at Arch Rock we were both lacing up for a grim route that was barely a rope-length long. I looked up at it, started laughing and said, "What are we doing cocking around on this pissant climb?" The shorties all at once seemed like a game of charades, a surrogate ritual for our rendezvous with the heart of the dream. There was no more putting it off.

The next day we climbed a long route on Middle Cathedral Rock—or started to. We gained a big ledge after a couple hundred feet, and spent the rest of the day looking across at El Cap—just opposite—eyeballing the various routes and talking about trying it "one day."

This was tricky business, working on the fringe of the Big Question: *When* do we go for it? Physically, we knew we could do it. But pondering that mammoth chunk of granite it's your mind, not your body, that shudders. We intently listened to each other's voice, studied each other's eyes, tried to reckon without asking how the other guy truly felt about it. It's a known fact that you can't look at El Capitan and lie at the same time, not about wanting to climb it anyway. So we didn't press each other, afraid the other guy might be on shaky ground and *try* to lie, or start mumbling excuses about why he didn't want to climb it when you knew damn well he did. He *had* to, or he was a coward and an outright fraud. By the end of that day on Middle Cathedral, the Big Question had grown and swollen between us like a festering boil. We'd have to lance it with the Big Answer if we wanted to continue as partners.

"Maybe we should have a go at it," Ron finally offered.

"Before it grows any more," I said.

There is a ritual all climbers perform before a long climb, and it hasn't changed much since gentlemen mountaineers plowed up Mt. Blanc in tweeds and hobnailed boots two hundred years ago. The ritual flows from the fact that the quicker you get through the formalities and onto the route, the less chance you have of changing your mind; and after hauling Harding's epic through my brain a thousand times, I wanted to put that all aside and get on with it. Big climbs are not casual business, not something done for the fun of it, and there are always ready reasons why *not* to go. So when the urge strikes, you move on it.

The ritual goes like this: First, you pick the route, then a partner. Then you both go down with binoculars and study the climb. A wall veteran can tell much by a good glassing; a rookie can only get scared. The devil may show you a little flea of a man on your route, half a mile up, floundering and flailing and hardly moving at all. You picture yourself in his boots, glance at your partner and go to the bar to drown the urge—if anything's left of it. If the urge is still kicking, you return to camp, spread a tarp out and, referring to the guidebook and any tips you've picked up from friends or acquaintances who've climbed the route, you set about organizing the mountain of gear.

Dozens of pitons are lined up side by side, according to size, like keys on a xylophone. Nuts are arranged, carabiners linked and counted dozens of times, slings tied and retied, ropes inspected, water bottles taped and filled. Then you stand back and stare at the gear. Then you stare at your partner. Then you go back and stare at the route some more. If you can still look your partner in the eye, you'll probably go through with it, return to camp, pack all the gear and the food into the haul bag and try to knock off early. And anybody who says he slept well, or at all, before that first big climb is either crazy or a liar.

We slithered out of our sleeping bags around four-thirty in the morning, and hiked to the base in the dark. The waiting before a big climb is harsh, but hiking to the cliff is the worst part of all. A few climbers are loud and won't stop yakking because the worm is turning hard and deep and their balls are up in their throats. Most are stone-faced and sweating the big drop. But the cliff, once gained, which you vicariously know so well, eases the stress and loneliness of the march. We started up at first light, hoping to get far up the wall that first day. The normal time needed to as-

▲▲

Haul Bag

Everything that you must take along with you on a big wall climb you must haul up the cliff in a bag. Keeping the weight down is essential. You might scrimp on food, but never water. Most climbers can survive on two quarts a day, though you could easily drink twice that much. Water is stored in thick polyurethane gallon containers, which are often duct-taped to keep the bottles from bursting should the haul bag get snagged, or skid across a traverse. Food is stuffed into nylon bags, and consists of anything you can eat without cooking—cheese, sardines, dried meats, canned fruits, nuts—the higher the calories, the better. Along with sleeping gear, everything is neatly packed inside a haul bag, which is bullet shaped to ease hauling over the rock, and made of an extremely wear-resistant material like Herculon.

Big-wall climbers do not wear packs, weighted down as they are with huge slings of gear; so everything needed to sustain life is in the haul bag, which at the end of each lead is winched up to the belay with a simple block-and-tackle rig. The worst-case scenario is to have the haul bag rip and to lose your provisions. But even if the entire lot survives the wall, most climbers tarry little on the summit, making a mad dash to the deck where they can eat and drink. It is normal for a wall, even a short one, to take as much as a dozen pounds off a climber, almost all of it water weight.

▲

cend The Nose was three to four days; we brought food and water for a day and a half.

From the start, Ron and I climbed like madmen, trying to quickly get ourselves so irreversibly committed we couldn't retreat, so the only way off was up. Up to that day, my typical climbing outing involved driving out to Suicide Rock or Joshua Tree National Monument, cranking off a couple gymnastic, picayune routes, then retiring to McDonald's for burgers and enormous talk. But El Cap was commitment with a capital *C*, and like most newcomers to the high crag, part of me kept yelling, "Get the hell off this while you still can." It was simple inexperience talking. And it didn't help that the ground kept getting farther away while the summit didn't seem to get one inch closer—an optical illusion peculiar to all big climbs. The secret is to stay focused on the physical climbing. If you simply cannot manage the climbing and exhaust yourself trying, fair enough. An honest failure never haunts you because the body knows no shame. But if you let your mind defeat you, if you bail off because the "vibes" are weird and you let fear run away with itself, you have not truly failed, rather defaulted, and it will nag you like a tune till your dying day—or until you return and set things straight.

At the 600-foot mark we gained the first big pendulum—a wild running swing right to the "Stoveleg Crack" (so named because on the first ascent, Harding nailed it using four crude pitons forged from the legs of an old stove scavenged from the Berkeley city dump). From the top of a long bolt ladder, you lower down about 60 feet, then start swinging back and forth. Now at speed, you go for it, feet kicking hard, digging right. You hurtle a corner, and as you feel the momentum ebbing, you dive. If you've chanced it right, you plop a hand into a perfect jam just as your legs start to swing back. You kip your torso, kick a boot in and you're on line. A laser-cut fracture shoots up the prow for 350 feet of primarily perfect hand-jamming, the wall as smooth as a bottle and not a ledge in sight, each lead ending in stark, hanging belays. The climbing went quickly, and by noon we were on El Cap Towers, a perfectly flat granite patio about 20 by 6 feet.

This was our first chance to catch our breath and take stock of our situation, racing as we'd been just to get there. I peered up and across and straight down, and images were thrown back that no climber can entirely fathom and to which no one in any language can do justice. "Holy fucking mackerel," I yelled. What a strange mingling of terror and exhilaration I felt gazing down at the miniature buses and cars creeping over a world we'd left only a few hours before, but from which we were now separated by a distance that could not be measured by any yardstick. I flashed on my friends in Camp 4, half of them foreigners, and marveled how the dream extended beyond local or even national interests, and how much more outrageous the *deed* was from the *idea* of it. If it entailed physical dangers, I reasoned, surely they were worth tackling. But there was no explaining away the shocking uneasiness of facing the distance outright.

Above the comparatively low-angled Stovelegs, the upper wall rifles up into perfect corners—like a cut melon. To our right looms the fearsome sweep of the Southwest Face, which at dawn draws fabulous hues into its keeping. There lie the world's most notorious big-wall climbs, and it's hard to imagine an arena where man has fewer claims and less authority. We were following a good, secure crack system, but no such thing lay to our right. No ledges, no ramps. Nothing but a chilling, 95-degree wall, a shadowy void damn scary even to look at. Since Royal Robbins, Chuck Pratt, Tom Frost and Yvon Chouinard first scaled it in 1964, via the North America Wall, a dozen other routes had been established thereon—and what epics this great sprawl of granite must have witnessed. From our ledge on El Cap Towers, it seemed we could hear the echoes of all the tense leaders who had once passed there—their terrors and doubts, hooking and bashing their way up the wall's overhanging immensity. And it seemed, too, that we could see their moon eyes glaring at belay bolts hanging half out of the gritty diorite bands, where a dropped piton strikes nothing but the ground half a mile below. A precious few specialists thrive on this kind of work, and they make the most curious study in all rock climbing.

We pushed on, traversing up and across the Grey Band, a nebulous stretch at mid-height that follows an intrusion of flaky ash monzonite. By early afternoon we'd reached Camp 4, a small recess of puny terraces below the final corner, which soared straight to the top, 1,200 feet above. Suddenly, the breeze died, and the cruel heat welling off the white rock stopped us dead. The next ledge was 500 feet higher, so we decided to bivouac right there, on Camp 4.

No longer absorbed with hauling bags and climbing hard and fast, the bivy was like suddenly finding ourselves becalmed after a typhoon. We dropped anchor, tied ourselves off tight to half a dozen anchor pitons and, clasping the rigging, gaped up and down and every which way, trying to get our bearings. We studied the topo map to reckon where we were, and what lay between us and the home port on top. We tossed off some small talk, sipped the precious water, nibbled sardines and cheese and tried to ignore the fact that we were marooned on a knobby, down-sloping ledge scarcely big enough to sit on, 2,100 feet up the side of a cliff, with 1,200 feet of heavy weather overhead. Exhausted, we eventually laid back and tried to settle in, rattled by the naked feelings dancing through our heads.

If wall climbing is good for nothing else, it's a sure way to find out, once and for all, how you really feel—not what you're expected to feel, or have been told or taught to feel. Slowly, you take on the stark, barren aspect of the great wall, and sink into the tide pools of your mind. It's weird and disturbing to see what's prowling around there, and you can't surface no matter how hard you try. Down you go, into the silences within yourself. Finally, you hit bottom and just hover there, weightless, face to face with those ancient fears and feral sensations that reach back to when man first slithered from the ooze, reared up on his hind legs and bolted for the nearest cave to steady up. It's very much like being insane, but far more intense because you're so aware of it. Mastering these feelings, the inner tension of being strung taut between fear and desire, is the fundamental challenge for the wall climber.

It is one thing to simply battle your way up a wall, jaw clenched, heart thumping like a paddle wheel. But to thrive up there, to dominate the climbing with confidence, to feel as if you *belong*, requires a transformation of character hard to accept for a young climber. Up there with Ron on my first El Cap bivy, it seemed strangely unfair to have to grow all the way up at nineteen. I refused (in fact, passed out from weariness), then woke with a start at the emptiest hour of the night, completely disoriented. I writhed a bit, and came taut to the rope with a jerk. My shoulders and head flopped over the ledge and I might as well have been peering over the edge of the world. Mother of God.

Ron, sitting bolt upright beside me, said, "We're in trouble, big bloody trouble." Only then did I realize just how high we fools had flown. Then Ron started laughing and when I looked over at him, with his grave digger's grin, I realized I wasn't looking at a young tough from Sheffield anymore. And all the tension we'd hauled up there suddenly vanished. I sat awake for a moment longer, voluptuous with fatigue, then fell back and slept the sleep of the dead.

Precisely why a young man should ever find himself up there in the first place is a question that has obsessed the public since the first man climbed the first mountain. There has never been and never will be a satisfactory answer, for the reasons vary from climber to climber, and most all of them issue from cravings too deep and slippery for words to really get hold of. The great Italian mountaineer, Giusto Gervasutti, suggested that people climbed from a need to live heroically, to rebel against limitation and universal drabness, that being lashed far up El Capitan was an affirmation of the freedom of the spirit in dangerous and splendid adventure; and that most of all, we were so high above the trees because here we felt more alive than anywhere else on earth. If you were so inclined, you could try to look beyond the poetry and right into the labyrinth of human nature, understanding that the vast majority of hard-core climbers are in their twenties. Throughout the ages a spirit of competition and challenge and a primal need for combat of a kind has always stirred in young people. Perhaps for some this need is sated on the high crag. There are likewise the subconscious curiosities about mortality, the overpowering urge, if you will, to unwrap the present before Christmas morning, to see and feel and taste something of the gift of death that awaits us all—not in some high-blown philosophical way, but on a visceral level equivalent to the basic elements of air and sun and water and stone. But I'm reaching here, guessing. The question can, in fact, never be finally answered, for each answer simply uncovers more questions; and that, I think, is the beauty of the thing. If nothing else, climbing is a kind of search that never ends.

By mid-morning on the second day, Ron and I were well into the upper corners, more than 2,500 feet up the wall and into the really prime terrain. And loving it despite the lines getting snagged, our feet aching from standing in slings, the grime and grit and aluminum oxide from the carabiners stinging our hands, the flesh barked and torn, shoulders aching from 30-pound slings of nuts and fifty carabiners. Our throats were raw, teeth gummed, lips cracked, tongues like rawhide because you can *never* bring enough water, neck and arms flame red, backs crooked from hauling the bag, clothes spangled with sardine oil and sweat-soaked from sun to fry eggs by. But we didn't care because *we were on El Capitan.*

From the start, all the way up to the bivouac, I found myself measuring my reasons for confidence against the towering danger I was in, most of it imagined. But now I had gotten above all measuring, and my mind had taken a backseat to savor the chase as my body frantically went about its work. Nearing the top, the exposure is so enormous, and your perspective so distorted, that the horizontal world becomes incomprehensible. You're a granite astronaut, dangling in a kind of space/time warp, and the exhilaration is superb. Men talk of dreaming Gardens of Eden and cities of gold, but nothing can touch being pasted way up in the sky like that. It is a unique drama for which no tickets are sold.

Other routes are steeper, more exposed than The Nose. But no route has a more dramatic climax. The Harding headwall is short—50 overhanging feet—and after a few friction steps, you're suddenly on level ground. But since Harding's day, some maniac had reengineered the last belay so that it hung at the brink of the headwall, where all thirty-five pitches spill down beneath your boots. It's a master stroke, that hanging belay, for it gives climbers a moment's pause at one of the most spectacular spots in all of American climbing. Cars creep along the valley's loop road three quarters of a mile below, broad forests appear as brushed green carpets and, for one immortal moment, you feel like a giant in a world of ants. Then suddenly it's over.

But it wasn't over. Ron had scrambled to the top, had hauled the bag and was yelling for me to hustle so we could get on with our lives. But I didn't move. I *couldn't* move. I kicked back in my stirrups and looked around. I didn't know why. I had never lingered before, always pressing on with gritted teeth, surging, fighting both myself and the climb to gain the top. Suddenly I was free of all that, of all the incessant rushing; so I just hung there and took it all in, and for the first time in my climbing career I seemed to fully appreciate what I was doing, how outrageous it was. Only by lingering did I get past all the sweat and vistas and paranoia and flashes of bliss, and only then did the whole disparate experience harmonize itself into a point of emotional symmetry and purpose.

The moment lasted about a minute. Without knowing it, I'd been chasing that moment since the first time I'd laced up climbing shoes. Yet even then, I couldn't really recognize the tune. (Some years later I was browsing through Bruce Chatwin's notes at the end of his book *Dreamtime*, and ran across the following paragraph: "A white explorer in Africa, anxious to press ahead with his journey, paid his porters for a series of forced marches. But they, almost within reach of their destination, set down their bundles and refused to budge. No amount of extra payment would convince them otherwise. They said they had to wait for their souls to catch up.") Finally I stepped from the anchor and stumbled to the top. It was not yet noon on our second day. No party had ever climbed El Capitan any faster.

Those first few moments on horizontal ground are so disorienting they hurl you into a transitional spin where little registers. A big wall is strong drink for a young mind. Few can handle it neat; most are hungover for hours, even days. Whether you've taken one day or one week, you are a different person from the one who started 3,000 feet below. I've heard of climbers hugging boulders, punching partners and weeping openly—some from relief, some sad that it was over. I've seen other climbers babbling incoherently, and I once saw a middle-aged Swiss team simply shake hands, abandon every stitch of their gear—ropes, rack, haul bags, the works—and stroll off for the trail down, their climbing careers made and finished right there. Ron and I only remember coiling ropes and bolting for the East Ledges descent route. As is virtually always the case, you never descend a big wall the way you came up, rappel the route you just climbed. That is far too dangerous and time consuming. Instead, we hiked along the rim to a low-angle, shrub-choked gully east of El Capitan that—after several rappels over short, steep cliff bands, and two hours of furious bushwhacking—finally leveled to the valley floor nearly 4,000 feet below.

We got back down to the loop road about two that afternoon, exhausted by the nervous depression that always follows a wall. As we stumbled around a bend, El Capitan came into view, backlit and burning at the edges. For all the raw labor and anxieties of the climb, it was natural that, all the way up, I should wonder if I was committing more to a venture than it was actually worth, if I was putting too much into too little. But if there is anything of a magnitude that can blow a person off his feet, it's that first ground-level view of a wall he's just climbed. Too little? The second we saw it, Ron and I stood in the middle of the road and gaped up at it with our mouths open. It looked about 10 miles high. And how long ago it seemed we'd been up there, and how strange, as though we'd seen it in a movie, or in a dream, and had suddenly woken up, half remembering what it was we dreamed.

There is so much in life one can thieve his way past, can wheedle over with guile and fancy talk, can skip through on the strength and efforts of others. But not *that*. Not El Capitan. Nobody can climb so much as one inch of it for you, so the victory is all yours.

Later that same afternoon, Richard stumbled into camp having climbed, in four days, the arduous Direct Route on Half Dome. Ricky and Richard climbed El Cap the next week. By the end of that first summer, all of The Bird's boys had made it up "The Captain."

The first Yosemite wall master was Royal Robbins, who in 1957 pioneered the Northwest Face of Half Dome the summer before Harding bagged The Nose on El Cap. Though Europeans were climbing big walls, and had for decades, their climbs were neither as steep nor as technical as those in Yosemite, so the Yosemite pioneers had to invent and perfect many of the requisite techniques as they went along. As mentioned, the achievements of the great wall pioneers rank as high watermarks in the history of adventuring; and no one contributed more than Robbins. He accepted no boundaries without trying to break them, and was both a genius and a great climber. The way Robbins climbed was not a heritage, or an improvement; it was a revolution. There was about his career a majestic continuity. He climbed like a champion, and even after he quit he still carried himself like one and people will continue to call him one as long as he lives—

and long afterwards if they understand just what the man did.

I remember wandering through his climbing shop in Modesto, California, in the early seventies, looking for old photos of Royal on the first ascent of the many walls he had bagged. I reckoned the hallways would be covered with them, but there was only a Byzantine-like mosaic of Half Dome in his office, and nothing else. He carried the rest around with him.

In many ways, Robbins is an enigma, and trying to get hold of just who he is, and what drove him, is like trying to shoot a moving target. The few times I was around him, I always got the feeling he was forging on in the hope of finding something new inside himself, something he eventually sought by kayaking treacherous rivers. Many of the wall masters who followed had something of this quest about them.

Though over the next dozen years I would climb more than twenty walls, I never considered myself an authentic "wall rat." I'd knock off two, perhaps three a year. A wall rat might do ten. And not the "trade routes" like El Capitan's Nose, where the going is straightforward and a fit free climber can really make time. A wall rat thrives on routes where the cracks are like breaks in an old mirror, where nearly every piton hangs three quarters of the way out of its slot, where there are no cracks at all and you must hook dimples and scallops and bash malleable copper and aluminum swedges into seams and pin scars, where a single rope length might take eight hours to complete and the whole climb, twelve days.

I didn't have the patience, or the mind, to do anything but dabble with these big-time "nail ups." Although leading scared me, it was doable, lost as I was in the function.

111

Belaying, however—tending the leader's rope, stranded in slings for days at a go—drove me crazy. The intensity of the belay is made so by the long silences. Once the leader is 75 feet out, you have to scream to hear each other. You're essentially alone, too much alone. A couple days of that and I had "summit fever," the overwhelming desire to get off the climb—and that's just when a wall rat would hit his stride.

When wall climbing reached its peak during the mid-seventies, Camp 4 was divided between the wall rats and the free climbers. We free climbers outnumbered the rats twenty to one: proof, they reckoned, that they were the genuine article, since in any community it's always the few who do the crucial work. There were never many rats. Their craft was too dangerous and required too much suffering. Exposed as they were to sun and wind and long nights dangling in hammocks lashed high above the rest of us, they nonetheless lived in a somewhat sheltered world. Their crusade—if you could call it one—had slowly turned in upon itself since Royal Robbins and the boys first climbed the first wall, the Northwest Face of Half Dome, in 1957. In the ensuing fifteen years the rats had become increasingly detached and self-contained, finding security and even safety of a kind in the yawning void that the rest of us would pass through only at the fastest possible speed. In a very real way their game was a drama in which they held fast to their outlandish roles, and seemed as bound by the fatalities of fortune as the protagonists in a classical play.

They called us free climbers "cuties" and "lightweights," athletic enough, but lacking the essential steel to manage days, sometimes weeks, stapled to a big cliff. And they were right. We free climbers were caught up in athletic, gymnastic pursuits, scaling rock using hands and feet, relying on the rope and attending gear only to safeguard against a fall. And yet the rats were always goading us to join them on some grim big wall.

Many of us *were* wall climbers—on a limited scale, granted—but rarely did a season pass when a hard-core Yosemite climber didn't slug up a couple of walls. So the rats' needling—which for me started the second I showed up in late May and continued till the moment I left in August—had a grating, cumulative effect because, to a certain degree, I *was* a wall climber. If I claimed as much, the rats would really pipe up.

"Fact is, Long, you're a pussy," some rat would inform me.

"And a faggot."

"At least he knows it."

"Fuck all you rats."

"Them are pretty big words, coming from a queeb like you." More jeering and laughing.

"If you were half a man, you'd saddle up with us."

And they'd start waxing poetic about some giant new climb up some giant wall that I knew damn well would embrace great suffering and labor and terror—for me anyway. Then they'd haze and bad mouth and dress me down a little more. No matter how badly my fingers were slashed or my elbows throbbed from too much free climbing, I could almost always brush them off. But if I was reckless enough to let my pride get caught up in the whole affair, if I felt I was losing too much face, I'd call their bluff (in fact, they'd called mine), and I'd find myself bashing up a wall with a couple of rats. Twice I got suckered because I couldn't sufficiently recall the epic I'd had the first time around—when a projected four days turned into eight; when I took a 60-foot fall; when we ran out of food and water the last two days and our urine turned brown and my vitals ached for a month afterward; when I wished I'd never been born, and swore off climbing forever.

Many rats were extravagant characters I liken to the wandering prospectors of the Old West—fiercely private and independent. They cared little for supposed glory, nothing at all for fame. Having their exploits publicized or praised was considered poor form because their game was like all obsessions: personal. However much they liked the hazards, toils and long silences on the high crag, their climbing went beyond liking in almost all directions. What made them rats was who they became when they were pasted high above the world. A few were rich, rebelling against comfortable limits; most of them were poor. They all seemed to do just a little better on the walls than on the ground.

Most rats had their share of things going wrong, which all seemed to come from the ground. So they'd jump onto a wall and for a week or ten days could get free of the ground, and the ground free of them. Eventually, the walls became their natural homes and their appointed refuge from a world that confused or annoyed them. A few were different. They loved the ground, but the high crag even more. Zorba the Greek used to dance to forget the pain. Yet when he was happy, he danced just the same. I think if there had been a high crag in Greece, Zorba would have been a wall rat.

Necessity determined that they'd haul the duct-taped water bottles, the porta-ledges and hammocks, the Gor-Tex rain flies spangled with patches, the Ensolite pads and sleeping bags with names sewn into them (rarely their own). They also hauled boxes of Milky Ways they'd pinched from the lodge store, and they hauled cans of peaches in heavy syrup, tuna in spring water, greasy foot-long salamis and summer sausages, Pop-Tarts, smoked oysters, Cracker Jacks, jelly beans and Life Savers to slacken "Kalahari Throat." And sodas that would explode when opened but cut through the gum that accumulated in your mouth after a day's climbing and so were treasured like diamonds. But it was the other things they hauled that said who they were.

Ron B. was an extraterrestrial buff, and he hauled pseudoscientific texts about flying saucers and alien sex. He'd also haul a pair of "4-D" glasses, ludicrous red plastic jobs he had paid serious money for that any sane man could have bought at a joke store for a buck. Through these glasses he could "see" the gaseous trails of Venusian ships. Canadians Hugh B. and Steve S. were two of the foremost rats in the business. One time (along with three cases of Moosehead beer) they hauled a bag of golf balls they'd filched off a driving range in Palm Springs. They teed up on El Cap Tower, a spacious, flat ledge about 2,200 up the cliff. Along with 200 golf balls, they'd brought a three-iron, a driver and a thatch of AstroTurf, and they spent a June afternoon banging great drives into the meadow below. Several cars were struck, windshields shattered. The rangers closed the road down for three hours and fanned out on horseback looking for a sniper. Cars backed up, overheated, rammed each other. Tourists fought. There were several arrests. The case was never solved.

Before he died soloing on Higher Cathedral, Joe P. hauled a hibachi up Half Dome and up Mt. Watkins. Russ W. hauled a small acetylene torch so he could "barbecue" franks. Along with half gallons of diet Coke, Charles C. hauled up a dozen Frisbees and hurled one off the wall each night. When he finally ran out, he grew bored, and led the last 900 feet of an extremely difficult new climb in half a day.

Jeff T. hauled a brass crucifix and a wallet photo of the Virgin, a fake Spanish doubloon, a slingshot and fifty marbles. I don't know why he hauled these things, or what he did with them. Bernie M. soloed the Leaning Tower and Half Dome wearing a yarmulke—partly from authentic devotion, partly because he was "so bald you could see his thoughts." Tom G. hauled a harmonica, a kazoo and a 10-pound radio on which he'd play the soundtrack from *Doctor Zhivago* till we were ready to murder him—and we would have if he hadn't been six foot three, two and a quarter.

They traded off hauling the bags, sharing the weight of strange lives, dragging up the wall what others did not want, including each other. They hauled the clouds and the rain and the sun pounding on their heads. They hauled thirst that would have killed a camel. Until an avalanche swept him off Mount Kenya, Dan R. hauled a medical degree up El Capitan. Others hauled scabies and the drip, smashed fingers and swollen feet, broken ribs and broken hearts. One rat hauled leukemia up El Capitan at least three times that I know of. They scattered his ashes over Washington Column from a Stearman biplane.

They hauled the very mountain, shards of it flaking off under ten thousand hammer blows and sticking to their faces and necks and hands, stinging their eyes, blinding them to everything below. They hauled the pull of the earth and they hauled the earth itself because they could never leave it completely behind.

Take Darrel H., known affectionately as "Cro-Magnon," a Canadian woodcutter and the most stalwart bastard ever to swing a piton hammer. He had one buck tooth and a face like a cigar-store Indian. His fractured speech was the most conspicuous proof that he was self-educated. If he wasn't, his teachers should have been flogged. He seemed to survive exclusively on malt whiskey and "branch water," as he called it, and at the wee hours he could always be found stumbling back into Camp 4 with a load on. The next morning, it was straight back to the hair of the dog that bit him. Whenever he had a little more liquor aboard than usual, some fellow rat would drag him off to El Cap, Half Dome or Mt. Watkins. It'd take him several days to dry out and hit his stride. The second he did, he wanted off the wall and he wanted liquor so he'd take over all the leading and climb furiously to get the business over with. By the time the team would "top out," Cro-Magnon was in mint condition, while his partners looked like they'd just crossed Chihuahua on bare knees. Then it was straight to the liquor store for Cro-Magnon, then back onto a wall, then back into the bottle and it was just one crazy, endless go-around.

They hauled the stress of men engaged in dangerous work and they made jokes about it. They hauled their honor with them, for they were its only custodians. Some hauled loneliness so deep and so treasured they would share it with no one—like "Private Dave" from Montana, thirty-something and heroically laconic, who always climbed his walls solo, which is twice as dangerous, three times the work and a hundred times more frightening. (If any man should feel like the last soul on earth, he's the one hanging alone in a hammock in the dead of night, half a mile up a big wall.) After a long climb, Dave would join in at every campfire, laugh and carouse with climbers he'd known for ten years. Then, slowly, we'd see less and less of him, until finally he'd start laying out gear on a tarp and borrowing water bottles. And where was Dave going? "Back to the high lonesome," he'd say, grim as a hangman, "where there ain't no people at all—yet.'' Private Dave preferred his own company, and up on the high lonesome, he and the work understood each other perfectly.

The sun and moon would come and go but time was frozen for the rats. They climbed a foot a minute—maybe— working toward the sky, hammering, always hammering, beyond willpower and resolve because it was all instinct, an emptying of thought. They had no commission and no guarantees, no boss and no pay. They took insane risks. They'd wander over vast oceans of vertical rock, seemingly with no scheme or objective, because the yawning void was their overriding purpose. Their quest was their religion, and in religion seeking is finding. In other ventures, it's the object of the quest that often brings satisfaction, or something incidental picked up along the way. But in the rat's theology, desire was fulfillment, and the seeking itself was its own reward. The summit meant nothing, the wall everything.

Eventually, some rats moved on to big mountains in Peru and Bolivia and Tibet and India and China, and many of them never made it back. Over time, the others ran out of Frisbees and golf balls, tired of Cracker Jacks and Doctor Zhivago, could no longer see anything through their red plastic glasses, could no longer haul a world of their own making. By twos and threes, the rats left Yosemite and for many years, the walls were nearly silent.

They were the genuine article. They hauled life and death in the same bag. The wall rats hauled with them a dream now lost in time, like the slipstreams of Venusian ships. Hanging bivouacs can get complicated, depending on the location and the number of climbers and haul bags you have along. Since porta-ledges first came into vogue, the process has been greatly simplified. They are rigged with

▲▲▲

How Do You Sleep up There?

When there's no ledge, you "sleep" in a small, nylon hammock, or "porta-ledge," that is lashed to the wall. When "hanging bivouacs" were first encountered, circa 1960, climbers used simple sailors' hammocks, mesh-nylon jobs as uncomfortable as they were flimsy. About 1970, specially designed "wall hammocks" became commercially available, but they too so squeezed a climber's shoulders that cutting quality logs in them was virtually impossible. Finally, in the late seventies, the first "porta-ledge" appeared—a one-by-two-meter frame of hollow aluminum tubes that could be quickly plugged together and covered with a taut nylon "bed." These porta-ledges were strong, light (7 pounds), stable and comfortable, and turned many a grievous night into a pleasant one.

▲

single-point suspension, and most of the time climbers simply tier them one above the other. If you're all on a steep, sheer wall, it's simple—you just clip off to the anchor, or to a rope tied thereon. But if you're in a corner, or the rock is peppered with roofs or other features, you might have to spread out horizontally, or wherever you can find a smooth section of rock to rig things. In this case, most climbers will traverse off to the side and place a provisional anchor to sling their hammock or porta-ledges from, while the main anchor (which is always bombproof, and to which you are physically tied off too—taut), mere feet away, provides the real security. You want to make sure the anchor that's actually supporting your weight is bomber no matter how good or how close the principal anchor is. If your hammock anchor fails in the night, you're in for a horrifying plunge

onto the main anchor, followed by at least an hour of grievous, pitch-black fumbling and cursing to rerig everything
while your partners laugh and shame you for your stupid-
ity, or curse you for waking them.

One of the most jackass fads that ever swept through
Yosemite passed in the late seventies, when wall climbing
was at its peak. I don't know which blockhead conceived it,
but for a while it became stylish to see just how meager an
anchor you could hang from for the night. Again, you were
backed up by an absolutely bombproof, principal anchor,
but what your hammock was actually slung from was as
dicey as you were foolish.

For a while (a short while), we'd all sleep hanging off
micro-pitons, slings looped over the merest bumps and
warts—stuff so marginal you couldn't sneeze without its
failing. There was talk that Hugh Burton once slept hanging from a skyhook, snagged on the slightest rugosity. Ten
years later, he told me he hadn't slept, so scared was he to
even wink, lest the hook pop and his reputation be ruined.

For my own part, I remember being halfway up a new
wall in the Sierras and slinging my hammock from a wired
nut the size of a peso. I was with Richard Harrison, who
sleeps like Methuselah's father, which is deep and sound;
but I've always slept like I was heading for the gallows,
more so when hanging from a harpstring and squashed into
a hammock designed for people skinny enough to shower
inside a barrel of a .22. And when later that sleepless night
Richard farted, or a carabiner shifted or something made
some such noise, I can assure you Lazarus dashed out of his
sarcophagus with less alacrity than I got the hell out of that
hammock and onto the main anchor. That fad was a short-
lived one.

*　　*　　*

"Crags," where the vast majority of climbing is done, are usually some kind of rock outcrop, and are rarely more than a couple hundred feet high, if that. A big wall rarely earns the name unless it's upwards of 1,500 feet high. So wall climbing is to crag climbing what the Indianapolis 500 is to hot-rodding dad's Buick. Every wall, regardless of difficulty, is an Olympic final, and anyone who achieves one deserves a gold medal. Few climbers ever make wall climbing their occupation, myself included. Nine out of ten climbers never take the sport beyond hobby status, and a trip up El Capitan, or up the Diamond, on Long's Peak in Colorado, often caps a career that the complications of work and family have checked to summer weekends.

One of the miracles of rock climbing is that for every severe wall, there are a dozen "easy" ones. No wall is really easy, for hauling a bag full of provisions up a cliff is always tough duty, and the physical demands and discomforts are roughly the same no matter how far the pitons go in. *Easy* only denotes that the technical difficulties are less. The arena is precisely the same—vertical to overhanging rock a long way above the trees. And since the psychological challenges also are so similar, an ardent recreational climber can get a solid dose of it without giving up his day job. That's why all wall climbers, no matter their level of achievement, are part of a hermetic community, for everything done on the high crag is of a piece. You can often find the first-time wall climber shoulder to shoulder with the veteran, both staring up at the high crag, both feeling the spell exerted by it; and to both, the big wall will always have the aspect of a daydream after ten beers.

The little crag is, and will always remain, the cornerstone of American climbing. Psychologically, there is an upward spiral leading directly from the small cliff to the high crag, a sort of vortex that sucks your imagination up the sheer rock and compels the few who make wall climbing their principal pursuit. These few men and women are the ones taking the big risks, sweating the big drop and grappling with mental hurdles that the rest of us cringe at. Wall climbing is much more a journey through the abyss of your own mortality than a contest against bad pitons and expanding flakes, and as a wall climber gains experience, the question becomes: How much of that death do you want to taste? If you are to truly thrive on the high crag, you have to let go completely and do battle with the Gods. Then you can revel in your own survival, a reward strange as it is real—cheating death, or feeling as if you have. I liked the surviving part, but could never let go completely, and so avoided the fearsome addiction and, to me anyway, some of the delusions that always seemed to follow.

Pessimism is the besetting disease of most wall rats. The tacit assumption is that life *is* trouble. Only death is not. And the only way to be alive, really alive, is to rack up, tie in and go *looking* for trouble. A cracking, eight-day epic becomes more real, therefore more legitimate, than horizontal living, particularly on new routes. Do something new and you are new, the thinking goes. The catch—if you keep at it long enough, and especially if you venture away from the largely manageable dangers and predictable weather of Yosemite (as most wall rats did)—is that you'll inevitably end up in an epic that will kill you. Or should have. The scenario always varies, but it's remarkable how the classic saga so often plays out along certain lines.

Most likely you've been looking at a lot of hard climbing, days of it. Then, the storm rolls in or the rocks start falling. You think you deserve a rest, and it's automatic to start feeling sorry for yourself—beat up, freezing, withered by

thirst or whatever. If you want to make it through, however, you can brook no "Why am I climbing?" sentiments.
You're in a war, and you have to fight. And you might die.
You're afraid, of course. Fear is natural enough. But you
can't worry about it, or yourself. You have to stop making
plans, forget about getting back to camp, consider yourself
already dead. You have to let it go. Completely. Only after
you do might you survive. If you can't, if you rate yourself
too high, with a special kind of hide to be saved, you'll stop
taking the phenomenal risks that are your only hope of
getting out alive. The other, rarer scenario is to short-
circuit from panic and, as Robbins said, ". . . die as a
direct result of being afraid to die." The numbers say if
you venture enough times onto the high crag, you'll find
your epic sure enough. And if you get through it, nothing
will ever be the same again.

But there's also the element of pure luck, or better yet,
fluke; and there's no explaining or understanding it. I was
on El Cap after a big storm, when the afternoon sun loosed
freightcar-sized ice blocks down the wall. I've also been
caught high on a new wall on El Gran Trono Blanco (Mexico) with Hugh Burton, when an irreversible pendulum
below us canceled our retreat and a windstorm kicked up
so violently that for two days the face was scoured by loose
rocks blown off the summit by the gale. How I got through
these journeys unscathed is beyond me to explain, but after
each one, the water tasted a little sweeter, the bed felt a
little softer, and my friends seemed a little closer than before.

Finally, I did one last wall on El Cap, a spectacular,
overhanging line called The Shield, then put my wall gear
away for good. Yet hardly a week goes by that I don't
wander back to those days dangling in slings up on Half

Dome or El Capitan or Mt. Watkins, knowing that some part of me will be battling up the High Lonesome for the rest of my life.

I'm glad to have once been there, more so that I never became truly addicted. I remember meeting British climber Alan Rouse years after we'd first met and climbed in Yosemite. I congratulated him on becoming one of the few pure rock climbers to make the transition into super Alpine climbing in the Karakoram and Himalaya. He chuckled and said, "The one thing that keeps worrying me about being one of the few is the way we keep getting fewer." He died the next year on K2, too addicted to quit.

To many experienced climbers, the high crag embodies all that is essential, grand, dreadful and true about climbing. The wild gymnastics of the short routes are thrilling, even remarkable; but they cannot lay bare, or even touch, that immutable stuff at the bottom of us. Such is the power of the big walls that, in a thousand varied designs, leave their brand on all who pass over them. Like the Swiss team I saw abandon everything atop El Cap and walk away, some men come and go; and the Tobins and Alan Rouses live and die; and the Cro-Magnons and Private Daves leave their memories. But once you set sail on the high crag, the long journey never really ends.

For perhaps seventeen years, American rock climbing had a crowning age—an era that can be defined by the ability of one climb to change the way people think about an already well-established sport. While it is totally erroneous to consider Yosemite the only place to rock climb in the United States, the golden age of traditional American climbing started and ended in the valley, running from about 1957 to 1975. During these years, American climbing (particularly the long wall climbs) was at the forefront, technically beyond what was happening anywhere else. (Free-climbing standards in England and East Germany were surely as high, but they lacked the big walls, so their endowments were more specialized.)

By 1970, wall climbing was so well established that, in the ensuing twenty years, there has been virtually no big breakthrough in the art. Refinements, certainly, but all the procedures, almost down to the last detail, have remained the same. For the staunch wall rat, the seventies were much more a time of scurrying around trying to pick off the last great lines than that of inventing a new art. The new twist, the last hurrah of the golden era, was the free-climbing revolution.

By about 1973, The Bird and his boys were in overdrive. We were continually amazed at how, in an area so picked over by so many climbers, The Bird could always come up with another masterpiece to bag. Jim Pettigrew said The Bird could have wheedled Old Nick into giving him hell if he'd thought there were any new routes to climb there. The result was that by the following summer, the sport was totally reoriented. Pure rock climbing had finally earned its position as an end in itself, no longer a sideshow, or a warm-up for the big mountains.

Climbing standards had risen so high and so quickly that only those wholly focused on the crags could hope to do the hardest routes. The new advancements occurred once leading climbers started taking a pure athletic approach, including aggressive cross-training and an itinerary that put the highest premium on time spent on the rock. Never before had so many climbers spent so much time on so many hard routes. Fitness, protection devices and boots improved, old test pieces were reduced to workout climbs, and the 5.11 standard, once the cutting edge, was now the norm. Then came 5.12, and free climbing had finally come of age. The 5.12 rating represented the 3.50 mile, the 90-mile-an-hour fastball, and to the few climbers who could manage that standard, there remained only one river to cross: Who would free climb, from bottom to top, a legitimate big wall?

The East Face of Washington Column was the first to fall, and quickly garnered the reputation as the world's greatest rock climb, a moniker hung on it by the great British climber, Pete Livesy, who made an early ascent with Ron Fawcett. The marvel of free climbing a big wall rests with the geological improbability of the project. The loose definition of a big wall is a gigantic chunk of rock, at least vertical in angle, requiring several days to ascend. Prior to the first free ascent of the East Face (later dubbed "Astroman," after a Jimi Hendrix tune), a bona fide wall was always a direct aid project, where climbers bashed and pitoned their way to the summit. To free climb such a route was miraculous not so much for the technical difficulties, but because if the cracks or holds blanked out for so much as a body length, the route would not go entirely free. In the case of Astroman's 1,600 overhanging feet, there was always a crack, or a hold, at the free climber's disposal, however scant or rounded.

The next year, the Chouinard/Herbert route on the North Face of Sentinel went free, then Quarter Dome and finally the Robbins route on Half Dome. The idea that free climbing was a gymnastic art for small crags was forgotten forever.

The greatest of the free ascents changed a few climbers' lives forever. But something else, which had nothing to do with climbing whatsoever, had an even greater impact on

Long, Classic Free Climbs
in the United States

YOSEMITE

Middle Cathedral:
> *Central Pillar—Grade IV, 5.11*
> *Stoner's Highway—Grade VI, 5.10*
> *Direct North Buttress—Grade IV, 5.10*

El Capitan:
> *West Face—Grade V, 5.11*
> *Salathea Wall—Grade VI, 5.13*
> *East Buttress—Grade IV, 5.10*

Upper Falls:
> *Geek Towers—Grade IV, 5.11*

Washington Column:
> *East Face (Astroman)—Grade V, 5.11*

Half Dome:
> *Regular Route—Grade V, 5.11*

Quarter Dome:
> *North Face—Grade V, 5.12*

Sentinel:
> *Chouinard/Herbert—Grade V, 5.11*

Rostrum:
> *North Face—Grade V, 5.11*

Few long climbs see the same traffic as the Yosemite classics, but there are countless other gems throughout the United States. The following list is woefully incomplete, and only suggests a few of the hundreds out there:

Red Rocks, Nevada:
Levitation 29—Grade IV, 5.11

Diamond, Rocky Mountain National Park, Colorado:
Yellow Wall—Grade IV, 5.11

Black Canyon, Gunnison, New Mexico:
Scenic Cruise—Grade IV, 5.10

Grand Teton, Wyoming:
North Face/North Ridge combination—Grade IV, 5.8

Cascades, Washington:
Mt. Stuart, Direct North Ridge—Grade V, 5.9

Sierras, California:
Keeler Needle—Grade V, 5.10

many of the same climbers: "The Wreck." Nearly twenty years later, a shamelessly embroidered version of the event would provide the basis for Sylvester Stallone's hit movie, *Cliffhanger.*

In short: One of The Bird's boys—call him Woody—was shacked up with a gal who worked as an operator on the park service switchboard. Through error or craft, she cut into the chief's line and overheard a conversation concerning a plane that had crashed into Upper Merced Lake, sixteen miles away from valley central, in the rugged and then snowy backcountry. Over dinner that night, she casually mentioned to Woody what she'd heard over the chief's line. Woody saw some potential here, for the plane had been identified as a Lockheed Loadstar, and he knew the nickname for such a craft: "Smuggler's Special." The next day, Woody's girl was eavesdropping the chief's line in earnest.

She quickly learned that the previous morning, two rangers had been dispatched to go scout the wreck (it was never known how the park service discovered the wreck in the first place). The pilot and copilot were found dead. Given the waist-deep snow and 16-mile trudge from the valley floor, the chief opted to wait till the winter thawed a little before conducting a thorough investigation. The rangers skied the two stiffs out on sleds, and the case was put on the back coals.

That night, freezing their asses off in Levi's and tennis shoes, Woody and two other Camp 4 locals trekked up to Upper Merced Lake to find the Loadstar augured into the frozen surface. With the aid of spelunkers' headlamps, they picked through the debris inside the plane, their legs stemmed out on twisted struts above a maw of icy slush (the nose of the plane was pointing straight up). When Woody reached down into the slush and heaved out what looked like a hay bale, the headlamps converged. They hauled the stuff outside into the moonlight, studied it under their headlamps, sniffed it, ate it and still couldn't believe it. They stampeded over one other and back into the plane and sure enough, the submerged fuselage was bursting with 5-kilo bails of high-grade Columbian weed.

Woody and the boys made three trips in as many days and weren't able to put the slightest dent into the vast payload. Each time they hauled out a bale, another one would bob up. Since there was obviously enough for every rascal in Camp 4 to get quickly and shockingly rich, all of the Yosemite hard core were recruited. (If nothing else, Woody needed a few dozen strong backs to hump his plunder out.) Anyway, in a matter of hours there was a virtual mule train of climbers making withering loops to and from the lake. Woody had his load out by the first day, then it was each for his own (though most climbers worked in teams of two and three). Some returned with upwards of 150-pound loads of the "red-haired" weed, a burden that fetched roughly $50,000 on the open market. "Hiking for dollars," they called it, and in a week's time, more than half a million dollars' worth of booty had been hauled to light.

The plane had broken up, and many of the bales were lodged under the ice some distance from the wreck. After the easy pickings (some 1,000 pounds) had been plucked from the slush/fuselage, locating the remainder was written off—till a climber named Quincy schlepped in a chainsaw. For several days he skipped around the rink, boring the ice with the whizzing saw. If a blizzard of green stuff shot from the chain, they knew where to dig. By the time the lode was "played out," the lake looked like it'd been host to an ice-fishing convention.

What followed the strike was right out of a Fellini film. My friend—call him Upton—was one of the first ones on the site. He probed the wreck for one minute, found a wallet with nearly $10,000 in it, turned around and walked—and kept walking, right out of the park. Forty-five days later he staggered back into Camp 4 with a full beard, a shiner and two bucks in his pocket. Gene found a little black book with Italian names scribbled throughout. He burned it on the spot. On the last day, Steve returned from

Fresno with a diving mask, flippers and a wet suit. After standing by a roaring fire for twenty minutes, he lashed a rope round his waist and dove through a hole and into the bowels of the fuselage. Good thing, because in ten seconds, his limbs went dead in the ice water; but when they pulled him out, he had a death grip on an attaché case full of greenbacks.

The fuel cells had burst on impact, and some of the weed was drenched in aviation-gas. If you couldn't smell it, you'd find out the second you stoked a pipeful, when a flame like a blowtorch would leap off the hooch. But even the tainted goods were pedaled off at top dollar, and that's when things really got crazy.

Tim left for Berkeley in a wheezing DeSoto crammed to the shattered windows with soggy hemp. Ten days later he tooled back into the valley driving a candy-apple red, convertible Cadillac with fleecy dice hanging from the rearview mirror. Butch rolled in on a chopped Harley. Hank showed back up in a three-piece buckskin suit, with a Scandinavian hussy who spoke almost no English, wore almost no clothes and fawned over him as though he were the Second Coming. He spent $800 in the bar the first night—even bought the rangers a drink (beer). Climbers who a few weeks before hadn't had two dimes to rub together streamed back into the valley and were spending cash money with all the nonchalance of a Saudi prince. Good-bye Top Ramen. It was steak dinners forever, and cognacs all around.

When the rangers put the pieces together, most climbers cleared out to avoid the grill. The months that followed— for everyone—are best illustrated by the "climbing" trip Bernie and five others set off on.

They took a charter to New York, and the Concord to London en route to Chamonix and the French Alps. They had big plans: the North Face of *Les Droites*, the Walker Spur on the Grandes Jorasses, to name but a couple. Later, they'd swing by the Eiger, once they'd dusted off the Alps. They got hung up at a whorehouse in Bordeaux, however. A week stretched into two weeks. They were still there after a month. In fact, they never made it to the Alps at all. The next spring, the five returned to the valley, flat broke and about 30 pounds overweight. I saw Bernie—now a land developer—last year and asked him if he regretted not banking a leaf or two of the long green instead of pissing it all away in a French bordello.

"What, are you *crazy*?" He laughed. "You can always make money."

Easy come, easy go.

The summer following the wreck, the Yosemite hard core set to their craft with a vengeance, as if rediscovering their one and only passion, their roots. And El Capitan was once again the focus. As free climbers improved and standards rose, the level of efficiency, the simple ability of a climber to get up a rock regardless of style, also improved, and people started climbing the walls remarkably fast. On the more straightforward big routes—those featuring lots of free climbing—super-fit teams kept provisions down to the bare minimum, hauling just enough food and water to sustain their blistering pace. The climb took on the aspect of an athletic event, a race. With the endurance to climb from sunup to sundown, and the technical skill to dispose of even difficult pitches quickly, many big walls were scaled in half the time thought possible only a few seasons before. Naturally enough, the question arose as to just how fast a team could actually go, and the summer of 1974 was dominated by attempts to answer that question with the ultimate statement: Climb The Nose on El Cap in one day.

At least four parties managed to climb well into the upper corners, 2,500 feet up the route, before heat, fatigue or darkness overtook them. I remember being down in El Cap meadow with The Bird, looking up at a party high in the breezy dihedrals. The shadows were racing up the cliff like dark ghosts, and clearly they weren't going to make it to the top that day.

According to Bridwell, the problem wasn't a lack of endurance or daylight, rather the refusal of a party to commit totally to the one-day ascent. So far, every team wasted too much of their time and energy hauling bags full of gear up the cliff—*just in case* they got benighted. They began the venture not believing in the project to the extent that they gave themselves a backup. All or nothing, The Bird said, or it will never go. And what was nothing?, he asked me. You spend a night without a sleeping bag and food? Big deal. Summer nights in Yosemite never got below 50 degrees, and thunderstorms exhausted themselves in an hour.

Bridwell, Billy Westbay and I started up The Nose on the morning of Memorial Day 1975, and reached the top with three hours of daylight left. Aside from three ropes and a skeleton rack of gear, we brought no haul bag, no sleeping bags, little food and a gallon of water. When we got back down to the valley floor, just as the moon crept into the night sky, I had the eerie sensation that the last chapter of traditional climbing was behind us now, and wondered just what the ensuing years would bear out. The next step would require either a giant dose of raw nerve, or a complete revision of the rules. These rules, the grand tradition of climbing, had a legacy of more than one hundred years, and before the movement that would flush all that heritage down the toilet could arise, the boldest climber of the generation stepped forward. His name was John Bachar.

The rules in rock climbing are (or were) more specific than those of mountain climbing. Rock climbers don't simply climb rocks, big or small, but rather climb particular *routes* up rocks. There also was a long-established set of ethics about *how* a climber went about his work. Someone had to establish these routes, had to make the first ascent; and once a climber understands the nuances of routes—to know what makes a bad one, a good one, and to appreciate the genius of a great one—he comes to realize that a route, no matter how natural, is a creation, requiring imagination, creativity and considerable vim to pull off. For this reason, and given the ethics that preserved the tradition of adventure, rock climbing has always considered itself as much an art as a sport.

Artists of any description define themselves by the manner and methods they adopt to express their views. The ultimate mark is, of course, to create something totally new. As 1980 drew near, the hard-core American climber was living off pretty spare rations. On the long-established crags throughout the country, everything conceivable had either been done outright or at least broached; and so long as climbers stuck to the classical verities, it remained a game of more of the same, nudging the standards up in tiny increments, filling in the gaps. Certainly, much remained to do on the new crags. Climbing had boomed, and entire areas, especially in the Southern states, were opening up for development. In these areas, the first-ascent possibilities seemed almost limitless. But bagging another first ascent is quite a different thing from spawning a totally new movement, ushering in another phase. And for a few short years, people were still sticking to the old rules.

After all the big Yosemite formations were climbed in one day, speed climbing became a fad. Teams vied for the quickest time up El Cap, shaving minutes off the previous record, making the first one-day ascents of other, harder routes throughout the Sierras, Colorado, the Canadian Rockies and so on. The game even caught on in Europe. But the contest remained one of refining an already established genre. The same went for free climbing the big walls. No matter what somebody free climbed, it was still more of the same thing, however difficult, remote, wonderful or bold the route proved to be. Then, John Bachar came along with the most dangerous game of them all—"free soloing," or climbing without a rope, a practice that would rattle the climbing world down to its roots.

Free soloing was not a new routine, but the technical standard at which Bachar soloed made it a totally different deed. For instance, Henry Barber's Butterballs, in Yosemite, was for several years a thin crack so desperate that only a handful of the world's best had managed it. Yet Henry's first ascent in 1974 was followed by such a meteoric rise in free-climbing standards that by 1980, Bachar had climbed the route without a rope. And nobody could believe it.

Scrambling unroped over easy terrain is a required part of climbing, particularly in the mountains, where speed can allow you to outclimb a storm. Many top climbers had long made an occupation of free soloing routes well within their abilities, with nothing but their mind for a belay. But to start soloing routes at the top of the technical scale, where one false move and the reaper falls, was something frighteningly new. In this, the Indian summer of the traditional era, free soloing would represent the last major phase.

Soloing has provided me with some of the sharpest, and

greatest, experiences of my life. Particularly on longer routes, the charged mix of fear and focus is indescribable. No one argues that soloing is climbing in its purest form. That so few climbers have died soloing suggests that sober, calculated judgment prevails over the naive notion of the foolish adventurer going off half-cocked. Some of the true legends of our sport have reputations fashioned, in part, from soloing. Still, while we laud these climbers, a definite taboo shrouds the game.

Difficult soloing is reserved for the full-blown expert, for those who eat, sleep and drink climbing. But even for accomplished soloists, the practice is a mine field full of clear and subtle dangers. There is the macho element. As Hemingway said of bullfighting, it takes more *cajones* to be a sportsman when death is a closer party to the game. But the venture requires so much precision, focus and control that while machismo might initially spur a soloer, only exceptional technique and mental steel can see him through.

To the experienced climber, much of the danger of scaling established routes is imagined. A lonely bivouac on a big wall forces a climber to ponder his own impermanence, but there are, in fact, few accidents on big walls because the arena is so inherently exhilarating that climbers tend to proceed cautiously. The wall rats take risks that to the novice seem suicidal, but the rat knows precisely what he can get away with, and has the rope and the gear as a safety net if he miscalculates. The free soloist has only his boots, a chalk bag and his own basic stuff. And if he falls, he dies.

Accordingly, soloing evokes feelings of mastery and command, plus a raw intensity that even a million-dollar-a-year ball player can *never* experience. And there lies the snare. Following a particularly rewarding solo, when everything has clicked, the climber feels like a magician. These feelings can actually foster a sham sense of invincibility. So it's not unheard of that a narrow escape is followed by an eagerness to push things just a tiny bit further, for desire is the sequel to danger. Soon, the soloist is courting doom, and he'll quickly find it if he doesn't back off. The whole insidious business is closely tied to anything that is exhilarating, deadly and fiendishly addictive. And if ego gets involved, soloing can get ugly, and fast.

When Bachar's soloing feats hit the general public around 1980, his picture, dangling high on some steep crag, was quickly featured in *Time, Newsweek,* and every other magazine interested in shock appeal. Shortly, other top climbers were pushing the soloing envelope, and pushing it hard. While the number of climbers had grown tenfold in ten years, the community of hard cores was still numbered, which greatly magnified the slightest jealousies. If climbers' egos were big (and they normally were), the soloer's ego was often titanic. Who else could do something that any person on the planet would look at in utter stupification? There is *nothing* as arresting as watching a soloer at work, for it's painfully obvious that he's gone if he falters not for a moment, but at all. Yet he is no fool. The practice is so technical that he survives only through the rarest kind of skill, and even rarer mental control; and he has both in large measure. The free soloer stands alone.

The vast majority of soloing was done strictly in private, and for all the right reasons; but a honed soloer could sometimes not resist the chance to flash his art on an unwitting crowd. As the legends grew, ferocious undercurrents of rivalry swept through the community that sometimes (though rarely) found release on the soloing circuit—a killing field if ever there was one. The ground is hard, and when a plummeting body impacts it from heights above about 25 feet, bones shoot through flesh and features are rasped off faces. At the base of long routes, the dead bodies of free soloers have been found so heinously disfigured that their closest friends could not identify the corpse. If the route is steep enough for the falling soloer to free-fall through the air, his body virtually explodes on impact; I still see some of them in my sleep. I mention these things only to underscore the fact that the practice of free soloing can be a lethal affair. The miracle is that more soloers are not host to the dead.

It all goes back to the old surfers' code concerning riding the big waves at Waimea and Makaha. If you were not out there for personal reasons, the code ran, you were going to get hurt. There's been too much silly talk about "soul surfing" and "pure" motives, but if you wipe all the doggerel off the code, you'll see a piece of critical wisdom chiseled there in stone: You take on great danger not to impress a crowd or to get your shot in a magazine, but only

Soloer's Credo

Never solo something you are not positively certain that you can finish without falling to your death. This might sound vague to a nonclimber, sort of like telling a basketball player to only take a shot that he won't miss; and we all know that even the best player will miss a lay-up sooner or later. The same probably holds true for the soloer, so the few who make a practice of this most fatal game normally favor the relative security of good cracks, rather than venturing out on the bald face, where only a toehold need break for the curtain to fall.

because *you* want to do it. Otherwise, your desire is offtrack and can override your judgment. Then it's a spark on the tinder, and the soloer might find the ground rushing up in a hurry. If the soloing fool is fortunate, he'll have a harrowing close call. Mine happened at Joshua Tree.

At speeds beyond 80 miles an hour, the California cops jail you, so for the first 20 miles I kept it right around 79. Tobin used to drive 100 miles an hour, till his Datsun blew up on the freeway out by Running Springs. After half an hour I was doing 90. Joshua Tree came quickly, but the stark night dragged.

The morning sun peered over the flat horizon, gilding the rocks that spotted the desert carpet. The biggest stones are little more than 150 feet high. Right after breakfast I ran into John Bachar, who at the time was probably the world's foremost free climber. He'd bounce around the country in his old VW van, abiding at whichever climbing area the sun shone the brightest. All climbs were easy for Bachar, and he had to make his own difficulties. He completely dominated the cliff with his grace and confidence. He never rattled, never lost control, and you knew if he ever got killed climbing, it wouldn't be his fault. It would go against all taste and would prove climbing was foolish and all wrong. You'd sell all your gear and curse God for the rest of your life—on aesthetic, not moral, grounds. Bachar had been out at Joshua Tree for about two months, and his free-soloing feats astonished everyone.

Two weeks prior, a friend of mine had "decked" while free soloing at Joshua Tree. I later inspected the base of the route, wincing at the grisly bloodstains, the tuffs of matted hair. Poor fellow had overreached himself by two shattered wrists, a broken pelvis and a fractured skull—and had gotten off easy because he came off low. If you're going to free solo, I remember thinking, you have to climb within yourself, never goaded by peer pressure or ego.

It was winter, and college checked my climbing to weekends, so my motivation was there, but my fitness was not. Straightaway Bachar suggested a "Half Dome Day." Half Dome is 2,000 feet high, call it twenty rope lengths. Since at Joshua there are no rocks even remotely as big as Half Dome, all of our climbs would be short ones, roughly 150 feet long. The notion was to climb twenty such routes, which would equate to 2,000 feet. That would give us our Half Dome Day.

In a wink, Bachar was shod, cinching the sling on his chalk bag. "Ready?" Only then did I realize he intended to climb all 2,000 feet free solo, without a rope. To save face, I agreed, thinking: "Well, if he suggests something too crazy, I'll just draw the line." I felt jackals running up and down my spine, and kept reminding myself that I was the first one to start soloing at Josh, and had, in fact, introduced Bachar to the art several years before. But the jackals kept running.

We embarked on vertical rock; twisting feet and jamming hands into bulging cracks, smearing the toes of our skin-tight boots onto tenuous bumps, pulling over roofs on bulbous holds, palming off rough rock and marveling at it all. A little voice occasionally asked me just how good a flexing, quarter-inch hold could be. If you're solid, you set curled fingers or pointed toes on that quarter-incher and push or pull perfunctorily. And after the first few routes, I was solid.

Our method remained the same: We'd climb a hard route up a particular formation—rarely above 150 feet—then descend via an easy route to save time and because down-climbing difficult rock solo is twice as hard and ten times as dangerous. After three hours, we'd disposed of a dozen climbs and felt invincible. We upped the ante to a stiff 5.10, or extreme difficulty. We slowed considerably, but by early afternoon we'd climbed twenty pitches: The Half Dome day was history. As a finale, Bachar suggested we solo a 5.11—an exacting effort even for Bachar. Back then, the 5.11 grade would move us onto world-class terrain, just a tick below the technical limit. I was exhausted from racing up twenty different climbs in about five hours, having survived the last four or five on rhythm and momentum alone. Regardless, I followed Bachar over to Intersection Rock, the "hang" for local climbers and the locale for this day's final solo.

He wasted no time, and scores of milling climbers froze like statues when he started up. He moved with flawless precision, plugging his fingertips into shallow pockets in the 105-degree wall. I scrutinized his moves, making mental notes on the intricate sequence. He paused at 50 feet, directly beneath the crux bulge. Splaying his left foot out onto a slanting edge, he pinched a tiny rib and pulled through to a gigantic bucket hold. Then he walked up the last 100 feet of vertical rock like it was nothing. From the summit, Bachar flashed down that sly, candid snicker, awaiting my reply.

I was booted up and covered in chalk, facing a notorious climb. Fifty impatient eyes gave me the once over, as if to say: "Well?" That little voice said, "No problem," and I believed it. I drew several deep breaths, if only to convince myself. I didn't consider the consequences, only the moves. I started up.

A body length of easy stuff, then those pockets, which I fingered adroitly before yarding with maximum might. The first bit passed quickly. Everything was clicking along, severe but steady, and I glided into the "coffin zone" (above 50 feet) faster than I could reckon. Then, as I splayed my foot out onto the slanting edge, the chilling realization came that, in my haste, I'd bungled the sequence: My hands were too low on the puny rib hold and my power was going fast. My foot started vibrating and I was instantly desperate, wondering if and when my body would freeze and plummet. There was no reversing any of this because you can't down-climb truly hard rock any more than a hurdler can run the 110 "highs" backward. The only way off was up. A montage of black images flooded my brain.

I glanced between my legs and my gut churned at the thought of a free fall onto the boulders. The little voice bellowed: "Do something. Now." My breathing was frenzied while my arms, gassed from the previous 2,000 feet, felt like concrete. Pinching that little rib, I sucked my feet up so as to extend my arm and jam my hand into the bottoming crack above. But the crack was too shallow, and accepted but a third of my hand. I was stuck, terrified, my whole existence focused down to a pinpoint, a single move.

Shamefully, I understood the only blasphemy: to will-fully jeopardize my life, which I had done, and it crucified me. I knew that wasted seconds could . . . Then the world stopped, or was it preservation instinct kicking my brain into hypergear? In a heartbeat I'd realized my implacable desire to live. But my regrets could not alter my situation: arms shot, legs wobbling, head on fire. Then my fear over-whelmed itself, leaving me hollow and mortified. To con-cede, to let go and fall, would have been easy. The little voice calmly intoned: "At least die trying."

I punched my hand deeper into the bottoming crack. If only I could execute this one crux move, I'd get an incut jughold and could rest off it before the final section. I was afraid to eyeball my crimped hand, scarcely jammed in the shallow crack. It *had* to hold my 205 pounds, on an overhanging wall, with scant footholds, and this seemed ludicrous, impossible.

My body jittered there for minutes. My jammed hand said, "No way," but the little voice said, "Might as well try it. . . ."

I pulled up slowly—my left foot still pasted to that sloping edge—and that big bucket hold was *right there.* I almost had it. Got it. Simultaneously, my right hand ripped from the crack and my foot flew off the edge: All my weight hung from an enfeebled left arm. Adrenaline powered me atop the Thank God bucket where I pressed my chest to the wall, got that 205 pounds over my feet, and started shaking like no simile can depict.

Ten minutes passed before I could press on. I would rather have yanked out my wisdom teeth with vice grips. Dancing black orbs dotted my vision as I clawed up the last 100 feet and onto the summit.

"Looked a little shaky." Bachar laughed, flashing that candid, disarming smile.

That night I drove into town and got a bottle. Sunday, while Bachar went for an El Cap day (3,000 feet, free solo, of course), I wandered listlessly through dark desert corridors, scouting for turtles, making garlands from wildflowers, relishing the skyscape—doing all those things a person does on borrowed time.

On the heels of this episode—and for much of the next decade—Bachar pushed the free soloer's craft into a realm that few have equaled and none have surpassed. Yet the more astonishing his achievements became, the more he and the climbing community came to odds. The sport was changing. Following the European lead, the new blood was more interested in ferocious difficulty than adventure. The notion of mental mastery, so manifest in Bachar's solos, was written off as an obstacle in search of the technical limit. Safe and hard, that's what the new climbers wanted, and that's the type of new routes they started creating; and John Bachar never forgave them for it. But there were other factors at work as well.

Painfully shy, John was never long on social graces and tended to make others feel uncomfortable around him. He seemed to take pleasure in keeping people off balance because in any crowd, he was always teetering a little himself. He was smart, but his intelligence had a shade of guile to it, and this sometimes worked against him. All of this added to his reputation of being different and difficult. Some climbers came to dislike him. A few hated him. Even the slightest rebuff could hurl him into an interior funk that would surface in surliness and behavior that was something more than just reactionary. If he didn't fancy someone's new route, say, if the climbers who established it had used techniques that John didn't approve of, he'd take the matter personally and several times actually pried the bolts out of a new climb with a crowbar—essentially erasing what someone might have spent weeks, even months to master. The bolts could always be reinstalled, but that wasn't the point. Words were exchanged more than once. There were several fights. Then John would head back to the rocks, alone, for his push and pull of emotions could only be harmonized through soloing. The rest of the world, it seemed, could go to the devil.

Soloing liberated him from the judgments—true and false—of his peers, and was his only answer to his critics. If he couldn't win their respect, he'd rile them, or blow their minds. He blew mine. Many times. And I knew he sometimes did it on purpose, which I thought was a shame. There was defiance in what he did, as though climbing with others might dilute his own brilliance. He would show the world how it *should* be done. If there was any joy in what he was doing, I couldn't see it—though certainly it must have been there.

When climbing began to evolve away from adventure and assume safer methods to protect the leader, it seemed to strike John that the axioms with which he had defined his life were being flushed. In just a few seasons, the age-old ethics became totally liquid, and Bachar threw himself straight into the middle of the new wave, determined that the currents of change would not flow around him. But, of course, they did, and John Bachar continued to solo, if only to remain apart.

My fallouts with John were as much my own fault as his, but they seem unimportant now. In spite of his trying nature, he was a peerless athlete who could look death straight in the eye and never, ever blink. And that was wonderful no matter who he really is and what people think of him. Perhaps his dreams and ideals were a little tail-first; but he was always ready to risk his life for them, such as they were. John Bachar was always seeking other rewards than the rest of us, and only he knows what they really were. Not surprisingly, John continues to solo, trying to find meaning in a world he did not make.

It is a terrible fluke that tragedy should strike during this writing, but yesterday morning, on page three of the *Los Angeles Times*, I read the caption: PREMIER ROCK CLIMBER FALLS TO HIS DEATH IN YOSEMITE. Derek Hersey, one of the great free soloers in the history of the sport, had fallen off the Steck/Salathea route on Sentinel's 1,600-foot North Face.

The route is considered moderate for a climber of Derek's ability and experience, which only points up the fact that no endeavor of man is as unforgiving as free soloing. Our only consolation is that Derek knew this as well as anyone alive, and he went out doing exactly what he most loved to do.

By 1980, a new generation arrived to find the fields plucked clean. By whatever means, a new generation is required to top the previous one. Ego and ambition won't allow athletes to simply repeat the same old stuff, even if *old* means four years ago. Records must fall, new routes be climbed, reputations forged and past masters usurped and left to graze on their memories. But the new generation found themselves in a quandary, and for several different reasons.

As mentioned about the more established areas like Yosemite, Tahquitz and Suicide, El Dorado Canyon in Boulder, Colorado and the Shawangunks, in New York, enterprising climbers had for over fifty years scoured every inch of the old crags for first ascents, variations, direct starts—*anything* new they could climb and hang their name on. By 1980, most routes even remotely obvious had been done, probably for a dozen years. The frustrating thing was that there *was* rock to climb, but not by the classical verities.

Simultaneously in Europe, particularly in France and Germany, sport climbing had caught hold, and local climbers set to work on the smaller, limestone outcrops that pepper the countryside. The nature of the rock—generally steep to overhanging, and often wanting of cracks—rendered the old ground-up philosophy impractical, if not impossible. There was no way a leader could start up a new climb unless the protection had been installed *beforehand* because no leader could stop on an overhanging wall, let go with both hands and drill a bolt. Often the rock was too steep to let go with even one hand, if at all.

The limiting factor was the traditional style, which had always claimed it better to leave a thing undone than to compromise the cliff, and yourself, with dubious methods. The climb was always qualified by the style. But the European climbers would have had virtually nothing new to climb if they had held to tradition. So they broke with it altogether, and started prerigging potential first ascents, first by toproping (climbing with a rope strung from above, thus eliminating all risk in case of a fall), to see if they were possible, then by installing all the bolts on rappel.

The nefarious bolt, which American climbers would risk broken ankles to avoid overusing, quickly became the accepted mode of protection. Likewise, the idea of spacing the bolts well apart, creating a route requiring nerve, mental control and a touch of the mad dog from the leader, was also scrapped.

These new routes were steeper, more strenuous, technically harder than anything before, and the new pioneers weren't risking anything but strained tendons in trying to climb them. The emphasis now was on explosive, gymnastic moves that were hard enough without the added onus of physical harm. Plus, the top-end routes were requiring that climbers spend days, even weeks, and dozens of falls to work out—endless hours hanging on the rope, or "hang-dogging," trying individual moves time and again until eventually they could string the whole sequence together with no assistance from the line. So inside a single season, it became de rigueur to place bolts every body length to safeguard from inevitable falls, producing an altogether new kind of climb—the "clip and go" route, where a leader need only a rope, a small rack of carabiners and world-class talent to complete the ascent. The art of placing natural protection—nuts, pitons and all the rest—was almost totally junked. It was all bolts now. These new clip-and-go routes had, in fact, finally reduced free climbing to a purely physical discipline, and had, for many, completely emasculated the enterprise.

▲▲▲

Clip and Go

The term clip and go has come to refer to the new-age routes as well as to the practitioners—"clip-and-go" climbers. The new, gruesomely difficult free climbs ascend steep and/or overhanging faces, and the protection is almost all bolts. The leader rarely needs to place any anchors (e.g., nuts, pitons) in the rock. The bolts are "in situ," already in place. Hence the leader need only "clip" a carabiner and the rope into a bolt, and "go." Sounds straightforward, but hanging by the fingertips on a 105-degree wall and fiddling with a grim "clip" is tough duty, and causes as many falls as the actual climbing moves.

▲

Soon, the practice became popular in the United States, and a tense and lengthy war began between traditionalists and "sport climbers," as the new generation called themselves—a peculiar title, since most of the "sporting" aspects of the game had been factored out in the quest for pure difficulty. Of the many things pure rock climbing inherited from the tradition of Alpine and mountain climbing were the notions of bravery, challenge, fair play, gamesmanship, sacrifice, victory—and the belief that the greatest routes required the greatest measure of all these things. So to many climbers the idea that someone would study a route on a toprope, would rehearse the moves and even install the protection *before* he ever tried to lead it, seemed like the most shameful exhibition of cowardice they could imagine: to surgically remove both the mystery and the adventure from the project, for you knew in advance all the things that climbers used to risk their hide to discover on the lead, "on sight." Most all of us had, in fact, dabbled with this methodology before. I placed bolts on a toprope at Suicide as early as 1973, and took a load of heat for it. I also inspected routes on a toprope before leading them—not so often, but enough that I knew the world of difference it made when I went to lead the pitch. And I also knew I was cheating, and usually felt small about it. And yet now there was no shame, no concept of cowardice, because the long-standing notion of facing jeopardy with your own innate stuff—a tradition that reached back to the first time a man set foot on a summit—had been completely forgotten.

In the classic sense, the more technically difficult these clip-and-go routes became, the less impressive they were. Personally, I didn't have problems with sport climbing as a movement, believing myself fortunate to have gotten in on the tail end of an era when one climb could make a difference. If the next wave of young climbers were to make their mark, they'd have to adopt a different set of rules. Fair enough. They had little option, in any event. But I did and do believe that the whole sport climbing game had become too fine, too perfect and too specialized, and my ambivalent feelings about dumping the adventure element in climbing will not go away.

The Yosemite tradition always dictated that a master climber's greatest pleasure was a challenge, and he would accept it in any and all forms. You might not fancy off-width cracks, say, but you wouldn't duck them to preserve your elbows. But many of the new sport climbers had never even seen an off-width crack, because the clip-and-go routes were strictly face climbs. They were specialists who did one thing superbly, but often required a special, made-to-order route to really shine, or to shine at all. Not one in fifty sport climbers had ever climbed a wall. That seemed a shame, for the psychological battles I waged with myself on the high crag were more memorable that the physical climbing on the hardest short route I ever did.

For several years, some crags resembled a war zone. More than a few traditionalists had initially and provisionally nurtured the sport climbers' bag of tricks, never dreaming the movement would, inside a couple years, completely corrupt the ethics that had so long been held sacred. Slowly, they realized they had sent something into the world that had taken on a life of its own, lost all resemblance to the original concept and totally ignored the originators of the idea. In short, they had queered their own game. So they started shouting at the deed of their own making, calling it back, cursing it, hunting it down. As soon as a new clip-and-go route would go up, a traditionalist would follow Bachar's lead and pry all the bolts out with a crowbar. Foolishness and chicanery raged in both corners, but the new generation wouldn't be denied, and by 1985, clip-and-go routes were the rage and the focal point of the entire climbing world—from Japan to Austria. It came as no surprise that after the jeopardy—and to some, the nobility—had been almost totally removed with the advent of sport climbs, the sport got about ten times as popular inside a few short years. Wall climbing became an almost-forgotten art. Climbers started migrating away from Yosemite and to the shorter, newer areas featuring harder, risk-free sport climbs. The glory years were gone forever, and anybody who had been around for more than a few seasons knew it.

Sad, nasty and silly articles started appearing in the magazines, often penned by spavined old bohemians claiming what a disgrace it was that the sport had gone down the toilet—an opinion that few accepted. The reason was that in terms of pure fun, the new sport climbs had it in spades.

Part Three

recently went to a revival house and saw the Disney classic, *Fantasia*. At the beginning of the movie, as the musicians tuned up in the background, the maestro explained that what I was going to see were the designs and pictures that a selection of music inspired in the minds and imaginations of a group of artists. The music was of three modes: The first kind tells a definite story. Then, there is the kind that, while it has no specific plot, does paint a series of more or less definite pictures. And then there's a third kind, music that exists simply for itself. Absolute music. For over a hundred years, climbing was about a lot more than physical movement. It stuck closely to the classical plot of how the sport played out. It was probably overdue that climbing—or at least some part of it—would try to redefine itself; and in the ever-escalating march toward absolute difficulty, sport climbing became like that third mode of music in *Fantasia*, climbing for its own sake, or "absolute climbing."

Perhaps sport climbing's main draw is its appreciation of pure movement unshackled by all the fetters of tradition. And, of course, it has the magnetic attraction of something absolutely new. But sport climbing is not without its limitations—namely, scope.

Understand that a clip-and-go route requires major effort to create. Somebody has to put all those bolts in, and this takes time—sometimes weeks. Plus, the difficulty is often so great that many days (several seasons, on occasion) may pass before the climber can work out an 80-foot stretch. So the bulk of most sport climbs takes place on small crags, bluffs and outcrops. Also, the preferred rock is pocketed and overhanging, a condition particular to small limestone, volcanic and conglomerate cliffs. The result is that many sport climbs are short and, to the eye, rather scrappy and unimpressive. Sure, you can gaze up at a 60-foot, 120-degree wall and marvel at how someone can ever free climb it, but people were never going to queue up on the road to cherish its splendor.

Most climbers didn't get involved with the sport because of the appearance of clip-and-go routes. In Yosemite, or the Grand Tetons, it is easy to understand why a person would climb, surrounded as you are by cliffs a mile high and magnificent. But from the outset, sport climbing never concerned itself with aesthetics, and eventually removed itself from nature altogether.

Once top climbers started thinking of climbing in terms of world-class athletics, it was certain the milieu of "proper" sports would enter the game—namely, outright competition. Though clip-and-go routes were revolutionary in terms of technical difficulty, they alone were not enough to utterly shift the paradigm. Climbing competitions were.

There is some question about where the first climbing competitions took place. California climbers like to think that the annual bouldering competition in the Golden State, started in the late seventies, laid the groundwork for the big-time events of the nineties. More likely, competitions evolved concurrently around the world. Eastern European countries, particularly those of the former Soviet Union, have held speed-climbing competitions for decades. However, there is no telling who was first to test for technical difficulty.

Around 1980, Europeans—particularly the French—began staging local competitions. The first meets were staged on real cliffs, a practice fraught with problems. Weather was inconsistent. Finding an appropriate trio of routes to serve in successive heats was nearly impossible. Holds would break, nut placements would change after manifold falls and so forth. The trend finally has settled—almost exclusively—on artificial walls, where the difficulty can be adjusted for progressive heats, and the steady flow of competitors controlled. Since these contests have about as much to do with the great outdoors as a canasta tournament, the impact on the sport, particularly in terms of attitudes, was monumental.

Staging such an event is involved and expensive. Accordingly, competitions are not mere showcases for the best. Most have become sort of all-comers' meets, as much fascinating social events as anything else. This is due to a lack of sponsorship. American equipment manufacturers traditionally placed emphasis on profits rather than in pumping serious funds back into the sport. There are exceptions, but without a lot of entry fees from casual contestants, competitions are, in the main, economically unfeasible.

Yet, in one important sense, the open format of competitions is a blessing. The more people directly involved, the better the event. I don't think competitions would have taken off as they have if they were merely spectator events. It's a good deal for all. In an era when different factions are increasingly polarized, these competitions bring people together and help defuse otherwise petty differences. It's virtually impossible not to enjoy yourself at a well-staged event, what with all the screaming kids and unleashed dogs, the thumping soundtrack, the buffoon working the microphone and all your friends falling off the 5.10a route, which is probably closer to 5.11e. It's a riot.

Serious regional, national and international events generally are reserved for experts. But as interest grows, even these elite events have started holding an all-comers' competition as well as the headline meet. The reasons are simple. Climbers are action-oriented. Sure, it's entertaining to watch Rocket Cullpepper glide up the 5.14 route as if it's a staircase; but if you've driven all the way from South Dakota, you'll want to sink your teeth into something more than the Cliff Bars sponsors are hawking on sidelines. Climbers want, and have come to expect, some action of their own, so almost every meet, regardless of size and prestige, has an open category for the willing. After all, it's the entrance fees that make the whole shebang possible.

Artificial walls and holds have evolved steadily over the last few years. The first holds were designed for use on practice walls. These evolved when weekend warriors built plywood "cliffs" in their backyards, bolting on assorted bleak holds and staying tuned with a little after-hours hand-traversing. Soon, climbing shops built practice routes on storeroom walls, attracting customers and attention to the sport. Universities started building large-scale walls for physical education programs. A whiskey distiller recently traveled the country with a few hotshot climbers and an artificial wall, promoting sport climbing and hard drink, and inviting passersby to tie in and have a go. But unquestionably the biggest boost for sport climbing has come from the increasing number of "climbing gyms" popping up throughout Europe and the United States. Most are built inside large warehouses, cost upwards of half a million dollars to construct, and are a far more attractive alternative the cross-training climbers used to do in health clubs and at home. In short, sport climbing has arrived. For better or worse, there is a whole cult of expert artificial wall climbers in places like Duluth and Key Largo, hundreds of miles away from the nearest cliff. Remarkably, some of these "experts" have never climbed on an actual crag.

The European competition circuit is promoted on a much grander scale than its American counterpart (twenty thousand spectators were at last year's world championships in Grenoble, France), so Europeans have more francs and deutsche marks to spend on custom-designed, indoor walls, some of which are not far from art in their structure and relief. In America, where climbing-industry money is in shorter supply, competitions have been staged on all manner of structures, including the sides of five-star luxury hotels and backpacking shops. Most recently, competitions have opted for a less-permanent medium—namely, custom climbing panels lashed to construction scaffolds, with the whole rig anchored by a massive counterweight to keep the wall static. These panels vary in size, but usually are about four feet square. They feature every conceivable type of hold—rounded nothings, underclings, side-pulls, comely jugs—the works. They also are machined to accept bolt-on holds, allowing each panel to be retrofitted to whatever degree of difficulty the course setter desires. A new series of panels may soon replace the old ones—one-piece molded panels so authentic in their rock-like relief that some climbers consider them better than the real thing. The holds are not bolted on but are part of the mold; some of these panels are bigger than four meters square.

Whether a big rig full of these panels will hit the road like a carnival act, serving every nickel-and-dime local competition, seems doubtful. Economics and practical concerns most likely will relegate the use of these super panels to climbing gyms and big-time regional and international meets. Climbing difficulty is altered by changing the angle of the panel. Unlike the traditional bolt-on units, these panels often offer more climbing options—move for move—than an actual cliff will.

No two competitions are alike. Some now opt to toprope competitors, rather than rig the wall for the simulated lead. Perhaps it's more exciting to see your buddy pay for his mistake by plunging off the wall, but sponsors are terrified of the notion that a competitor might catch his toe on the cord, spin upside down and smack his bean on the wall.

Since competitions are geared toward determining technical proficiency, the idea that elapsed time should figure into things is questionable. If two climbers flashed the final climb, some early competitions determined the winner by the elapsed time. Not good, since both climbers scaled the thing. To be eliminated because you were a fraction slower than Jose has led some victims to feel they've been jobbed— and rightly so. Accordingly, timing ascents has, for the most part, been done away with. Most often, if you flash the route, you advance. This system presents some problems, however. Competitions routinely run long, given the various heats. Sometimes there are hundreds of contestants. A recent solution, and perhaps the only viable one for a big event, is to give each contestant an allotted time to complete the route—not so little that it requires speed climbing, but not so much that one climber can bog the show.

The first competitions were loose, ill-defined affairs marred by scandalous judging and national prejudices. The Union Internationale des Associations D'Alpinisme (UIAA), a European-based climbing organization, now has a Competitions Committee (CICE) that makes rules for and oversees international competitions. In the United States, the member organization of the CICE is the American Sport Climbers Federation (ASCF), which sanctions local, state, regional and national competitions. In addition, the ASCF chooses a national team for representation at international events, and provides a training program for judges.

The ASCF focuses its efforts in two ways: sanctioning competitions for organizers and providing a numerical ranking for climbers. Competitors gain points at local and regional competitions that allow them ultimately to compete for a place on the national climbing team. Such point ranking also allows potential sponsors of climbers to see how good they really are.

(Membership in the ASCF is available at several levels. An individual who wishes to compete and gain standing can join for $25. Anyone with an interest in organizing or competing can reach the ASCF at 125 West 96th Street, #1D, New York, NY 10025.)

As basic as it seems, the best preparation for climbing on artificial walls is to climb artificial walls. The climbing resembles actual rock climbing, of course, but it differs enough that someone familiar with ascending artificial walls has a distinct advantage over someone who isn't. Those serious about competition often construct hand traverses— using the artificial holds—in their backyards, and practice regularly on them. In many areas, climbers have constructed "urban crags" by bolting holds onto convenient walls or bridges—even onto the undersides of freeway overpasses. One area in Pasadena, California, is host to concrete climbs upwards of 60 feet tall. Spending time on these artificial structures not only keeps your fingers tuned for the crags, but will familiarize you with the feel of competition walls. And avoiding the authorities, who want to know who the hell bolted all that crap onto state property, also can add some thrill to the venture.

With the exception of "elite" competitions, prize money is so nominal that the sport could hardly be called a professional industry. Even the foremost competitive climbers in America have to chase their tails trying to make a go of it. Equipment manufacturers will latch onto a champion, squeezing the last drop of promotional value from him or her; but rarely do they pay "their" climbers a professional salary (for rarely do they have it). For the casual sport climber, or even the serious one, it's best to consider the whole thing an amateur sport. If you win a rope, or a couple hundred bucks, great. If you don't, there's still no excuse not to enjoy yourself. And that should be the goal for anyone interested in competing: having a good time. Don't fret if you pitch off on the first heat. There will always be another competition. And of course, each competition has a handful of dead-serious competitors who look as though they've just survived fifty days at sea in a life jacket. With .01 percent body fat, their keen faces drawn and pinched, you hope they win so they can finally enjoy a square meal.

▲▲▲

Lynn Hill, Three-Time World Champion, On Competitions

Competition was a driving force in climbing long before the first organized meets took place. Climbers the world over always have strived to climb faster, higher, in better style, without bottled oxygen, etc. In so doing, climbers have competed against one other, against the rock or mountain and always against themselves.

Initially, organized competitions stirred a great controversy among many top European and American climbers; for various reasons, many of these climbers boycotted the first big competition, held in Bardonecchia, Italy, in 1985. Once climbers understood that competitive climbing was a separate game that neither infringed nor demeaned climbing on natural rock—and that there was money to be made—most holdouts chose to compete in the second annual Sport Rocchia competition, also held in Italy, in 1985. This was my first experience in a free-climbing competition.

This 1985 competition showed how hard it was to organize and structure a fair and consistent venue to measure performance. It could hardly be otherwise for a new sport, and I was not surprised that the rules and format were vague and poorly thought out. I was completely shocked, however, when the meet organizers changed the rules to enable a well-known European climber to win.

There were other disturbing aspects of this competition as well. The match was held on a cliff some way off the road, and hundreds of spectators completely ravaged the verdant hillside getting there. From the base, the viewing was excellent, because all the trees had been chopped down. The rock was trashed as well: holds were chipped, pockets were plugged up with cement, all to create routes of the desired difficulty.

Though they should have been the primary impetus, environmental considerations did not spur on the development of artificial walls specifically designed for competitions. Rather, bad weather, convenience of location (for spectators and the media) and the ease of fashioning fair and perfectly tailored routes quickly made artificial walls the preferred medium for virtually all competitions.

Despite the refinements in design, artificial walls are by no means a perfect simulation of natural rock, nor is climbing in a competition comparable to climbing with friends at a favorite crag. Competitions and artificial walls are simply another facet of climbing, one that provides a new form of play, fresh challenges and a novel kind of learning experience. As a result of competing, I have learned much about myself with respect to the psychological elements of the game, while my actual climbing prowess has steadily improved.

I can't leave off competitions without reviewing what is quickly becoming the showstopper of most venues that feature it: speed climbing. First seen in Eastern European countries, speed climbing has become an increasingly important part of many American competitions, depending on the size and timetable of the meet. In most competitions, a lack of time means organizers are hard-pressed to get all the contestants up the wall. But if time and facilities allow, a special speed-climbing event will generate a lot of interest and rave reviews. From a spectator's point of view, speed climbing is far more exciting than the technical event.

The courses usually are set up to allow rapid passage, featuring long and wild dynamic climbing between jug holds. Get a mad-dog speed climber chomping at the bit, goaded on by a couple thousand pushy spectators and the joker on the mike, and watch out. The 100-yard dash has got nothing over this event.

It's ironic that the term *adventure climbing* would ever be coined. Prior to about 1980, virtually all climbing was an adventure. Certainly, a climber could stitch a crack with nuts, or stick with relatively harmless, low-angled routes; but on the main, doubt, commitment, jeopardy and a major dose of both fear and exhilaration were the things that vitalized the game.

For much of the eighties, climbing magazines were full of the ongoing debate—whether the reigning climbing paradigm should or should not be dominated by short sport climbs. There were many from the old school who hated to see the icons they had forged reputations on summarily dismissed, while young climbers reveled in the freedom of a new game. The new stars weren't buying into the old credo—that active climbers must tackle the longer routes or they weren't "real." Never mind the macho posturing and pretense in such a credo, the old masters had a point: The task of climbing a long route not only requires more from the climber (chiefly, a testing of spirit), but it also offers greater rewards in terms of intensity and lasting memories. Climbers who limited themselves strictly to clip-and-go routes were depriving themselves of much of the finest that climbing has to offer, namely, the sporting aspect.

Take the Chouinard/Herbert route on the North Face of Sentinel, in Yosemite. It's a standard long, hard, free route. You're half trashed by the time you hump up the two miles of scree and grassy terraces to the base. The first thousand feet of actual climbing is mainly 5.9 and 5.10, with a touch of 5.11 to keep you honest. Then, the wall suddenly rears. A nasty 5.11 stemming job ends at a sling belay where you know you're on a Yosemite wall. Then, the leader underclings out a hatchet flake, 2,000 feet of air below his boots, pulls over a roof and pumps up extreme ground, afraid to fall because the protection is questionable. The belayer's is gripped. You'll remember those moments, and will savor them more than the time you cranked an impossible move 10 feet off the ground with a bolt at your waist.

The term *sport climbing*, which first surfaced in the seventies, originally did not mean what it came to mean later. Sport climbing referred to approaching the traditional climbing game from the orientation of a serious athlete. It did not refer to ignoring age-old rules in search of higher numbers. The generic, everyday usage of *sport* usually refers to certain physical games; and the thing that makes these games so interesting is the spontaneity of the endeavor—the running back's on sight read of the defense, the surfer's quick negotiation of the curl of a terrible pipeline tube, the Grand Prix cyclist's intuitive glide into a turn at 140 miles an hour. When watching a sport climber attempt a 50-foot route for the fiftieth time, clipping a bolt every five feet, more than one observer has wondered where the hell the sport is in such a venture. As mentioned, most of the clip-and-go routes are not sporting at all, rather they are remarkable examples of a physical discipline.

However, the climbing community has never made the mistake of putting absolute precedence on this form of climbing, has never supported the false notion that sport climbing was the best and only mode. Moreover, climbers usually made certain that sport climbing, distinct and valid as it is, never encroached on adventure climbing. They were generally mature enough to realize and respect the notion that all climbs are not the same. Basically, many climbers who were strictly sport climbers said jeopardy was not part of their game. Theirs was about doing hard moves, period.

Perhaps the ultimate irony is that beginning and intermediate climbers are the people who keep adventure climbing alive. Because the new sport climbs are technically far beyond casual climbers, the latter are left to cut their teeth on the old-style, traditional routes. So while a handful of the climbing elite concentrate wholly on pushing the technical limit, the bulk of climbers continue on as they have for many generations—climbing a route from the ground up, on sight, and placing all the protection as they go along.

As a general maxim, the more rules you impose upon yourself, the more you will get out of your climbing. This is even more the case when you take on a climb that, owing to its magnitude, isolation, exposure and so on, places severe restrictions on your method of ascent. The route need not have staggering numbers to provide you with some lasting memories. As fun and challenging as clip-and-go routes are, sticking strictly with this medium breeds tedium. Once in a while, a climber needs a baptism in fear and exhilaration, needs to venture out where certain things are beyond his immediate control. Get onto something long and wild, where you take things as they come. When you see big-name sport climbers free soloing, speed climbing big walls or climbing in wilderness areas, they're doing nothing more than this—jamming out to Zion, or Moab, driving a junker down to Mexico and climbing at Trono Blanco, hitching up to the Wind Rivers.

To the relief of many old-timers, wall climbing and long routes have enjoyed a recent resurgence. In a sort of inverse progression, climbers raised on clip-and-go routes slowly grew into the longer routes and rediscovered a whole new aspect of climbing that had been largely ignored for nearly a decade. All told, I think the detour into sport climbing has enriched the game, and now that more climbers are setting their sights beyond an indoor climbing wall, it looks as though the sport of kings is starting to come full circle.

In working through these pages I wanted to gaze back on my formative years without romancing the folly or reviling the clean thrill of climbing the big rocks, but this, I know, is impossible, since memory is a devil and the experience here evoked was special and exotic by any measure. Maybe it's because those years are gone and I can never have them back, but I can't help but ask myself: What did it really mean, how do I really feel about those years grappling up the high crag?

I'm dismayed yet almost relieved that I have no useful answer. If the answers were known, I might not be writing at all. We riffle through the chaos of the past and in the pure light of time, every crumb and every shard has changed because *we* have changed. Perhaps the true substance of those years is conceded by what I will always be—first and always a rock climber; and that goes back to Yosemite, more a state of mind than a place, a dream realm that part of me has never really left.

Yosemite climber Eric Beck once said that at both ends of the social spectrum there lies a leisure class. *Free* might have been more apt than *leisure*, though there's little questioning where in the spectrum we climbers lay. Yet many active climbers of my generation found it difficult to move on to fields of green money, families, mortgage payments and routines. A few never did. The initial move away was the toughest.

I remember when Lord Jim settles in amongst Bugis tribesmen, having found some peace of mind after years of desperate roving, and another European asks him about leaving. "Leaving!" Jim says. "To where? What for? To get what?" The hard-core Yosemite climber was worlds away from lordship; but at the height of the Yosemite heydays, had you asked any of us about leaving you would have gotten Lord Jim's answer to the letter. After all, to a fanatical climber, what was money and security, which added nothing to the beauty of his land or the life of his soul? If to have these you had to part with your native domain, which was to you the quintessence of all joy, poetry, art, religion, paradise, what was the point? Everyone else seemed so harried and chased, and the better they got at saving time, the less they seemed to have. It was all a delusion, perhaps, but snug in Yosemite, we believed it, and so for a time it was true for us. But, of course, life goes on, and you either hop aboard or get left behind in no-man's-land, which is as tragic as if you had never tied into a rope at all. The problem is, you need a reason to leave.

Mine came early one morning, following a bleak and scorching week thrashing up a new route on Mt. Watkins. Stumbling back to Camp 4, I saw all the ratty haul bags strung from trees, the stacks of filthy cooking gear atop filthy picnic tables, and the climbers—my dearest and only friends—scruffy as felons, slithering from tumble-down tents pitched straight in the dirt; and I realized what a dog's life I'd been leading—*was* leading— after all.

I got over the feeling—for a while. Another big climb set things straight quickly enough. But the thin end of the wedge had been set. One day I reached into my pocket and found I didn't have ten bucks to my name. It never mattered before. But the grubby fact of my poverty had, in fact, jumped into my awareness that morning as I stumbled through camp. Unconsciously, I was scared and humiliated, and slowly came to regard with sympathetic shame the same condition in my friends. When I realized that the shame was my own, I was through. The valley walls squeezed in on me, and a way of life I had savored for eight years seemed less like genuine freedom, and more like a one-dimensional vice with all the narrowness, futility and delusions of San Quentin. I lived in a social vacuum, on a cultural dune. I was, in fact, just a celebrated bum. After all the years of huge daily denial, the temptation to lead if not a normal life, at least a *different* life, was simply too strong. Plus there were those questions about how much I had betrayed that ideal conception of one's life that all people secretly set up for themselves. I wasn't alone in my thinking. Eventually, each of us asked that question old as Adam: What the hell am I doing here?

Utopia is a Greek word meaning "no such place." Once

I owned up to that fact, leaving the valley of my dreams was a lot easier. So it was good-bye to what had become a radiant arroyo named Yosemite and on to see the big world. I went to the North Pole, ran with the Pamon in the Venezuelan rain forest, shot rivers in Borneo, caved in Papua, kayaked the Solomons and never once found the intensity I used to feel climbing in the valley.

It has been many years since I dreamed of nothing but climbing rocks. But last year I passed through Yosemite. I hadn't been there for a long time. When you return to a place where you fooled away your youth, you find that some of it has remained important. But if you go back to the old creek, or the baseball diamond, you're sobered by how small it all seems. Not so, Yosemite. I walked down to El Cap meadow early one morning and was more amazed than ever by how *big* the walls looked. It seemed miraculous that I ever got up a few of them.

Then, I saw a man, old and tired, leaning against a tree and staring up at El Capitan. And that old man was I. His face was seamed and toothless, but he was pleased to recognize his face in mine, and to remember all the other faces, faces in Camp 4, faces of friends. Each passing year, shadows obscure them, and eventually their greatest climbs will strike the ear like antique battles until someday, their Rubicons and Waterloos will be forgotten forever. But in ten thousand years El Capitan will still rise, white and bold, and the little shady patch of dirt and pine needles and gray boulders we knew as Camp 4 will still be there. And if people are still climbing then, still hanging in the old Camp 4, I hope one of them will sit down among the boulders and listen to the muted echoes of all those who used to live and climb there. Nobody before or since has felt their lives more acutely, and their stories are worth hearing.

Glossary
of Common Terms

AID: using means other than the action of hands, feet and body English to get up a climb

ANCHOR: a means by which climbers are infallibly secured to the cliff

ARÊTE: an outside corner of rock

ARMBAR, ARMLOCK: a means of wedging the upper body into a crack

BELAY: procedure of securing the climber by use of the rope

BOLT: an artificial and permanent anchor placed in a hole drilled for that purpose

BUCKET: a handhold, large enough to fully latch onto, like the lip of a bucket

CAM: to lodge in a crack by use of counterpressure; that which lodges

CARABINERS (aka, biners, snaplinks): aluminum alloy rings equipped with a spring-loaded gate

CEILING: an overhang of sufficient size to loom overhead

CHALK: gymnastic chalk (carbonate of magnesium), carried by climbers in a small nylon bag at the waist into which the hands are often dipped—eliminates sweaty palms and fingers, and greatly increases grip

CHOCKSTONE: a rock lodged in the crack; now often also refers to nuts

CLEAN: a description of routes (climbs) that may be variously free of vegetation, loose rock or even the need to place pitons; also the act of removing gear from the crack

CRUX: the most difficult section of a climb or "pitch"

DECK: the ground

DIHEDRAL: (aka open book): an inside corner

DIMPLE: a tiny irregularity on the surface of the rock

DRAG: usually used in reference to the resistance of rope as it moves through carabiners

DYNAMIC: lunge move

EXPOSURE: that relative situation where a climb has particularly noticeable sheerness

FLAKE: a wafer of rock, the running edge of which is separated from the main rock wall; flakes can vary in size from small shards to colossal features hundreds of feet long

FLASH: to climb a route on your first try, no falls

FREE CLIMBING: to climb using hands and feet only; the rope and attending gear are only used to safeguard against a fall, not for upward progress

JUGHOLD: a hold that is like a jug handle

JUMARS: clamplike devices that fit onto a rope and are clipped off with stirrups; they slide *up*, but not down, and enable a climber to ascend a rope

LEAD: to be first on a climb, placing protection in the rock to secure the rope, and the climber, to the cliff in the event of a fall

LIEBACK: a climbing maneuver that entails pulling with the hands while pushing with the feet

LINE: the path of weakness up a cliff that delineates the route

MANTEL: a climbing maneuver used to surmount a single feature above one's head

MOVE: movement; one of a series of motions necessary to gain climbing distance

NUTS: (aka chockstones, or simply chocks): metal wedges of various sizes and designs, strung with cable or rope, that fit into constrictions or cavities in the rock. As of the late seventies, because of advances in design, the ease of use and their low ecological impact, nuts have virtually replaced pitons as the means of protection

ON SIGHT: to climb a route without prior knowledge or experience

PENDULUM: a climbing maneuver that entails swinging from the anchored rope to a hold too difficult to climb to

PITCH: the section of rock between belays; a rope length

PITONS (aka pins, pegs): metal spikes of various shapes that are hammered into the rock to provide anchors

PLACEMENT: the actual position of a nut or other anchor

PROTECTION: the anchors used to safeguard the leader

RAPPEL: to descend using a rope by means of a mechanical brake device

RUNOUT: the distance between two points of protection

SCALLOP: a tiny irregularity on the surface of the rock

SKYHOOK: a strip of steel crooked like a finger that can be "hooked" on small nubbins and edges of rock to support the weight of an aid climber, a dicey device to use, though routinely employed on long aid climbs

SLING (aka runner): a loop of nylon webbing used for a variety of purposes to anchor to the rock

SPORT CLIMB: normally a steep, safe, difficult face climb that is protected entirely with bolt anchors, where the emphasis is on pure difficulty

STANCE: a standing rest spot, often the sight of the belay

TOPROPE: a rope, usually doubled through an anchor on top of a given climb. One end is secured on the ground, the other is tied into the climber. As the climber works up the rock, the slack is taken in. Since the rope is running through an anchor on top, the climber cannot "fall," but will only slip back onto the rope. Toproping is a common way to eliminate all risk and free up a climber to concentrate solely on the climbing

TRAVERSE: to move sideways, without altitude gain